Out of the Depths

A Woman's Journey toward Wholeness

Judy Roberts

5 Fold Media
Visit us at www.5foldmedia.com

Out of the Depths, A Woman's Journey toward Wholeness
Copyright © 2013 by Judy Roberts
Published by 5 Fold Media, LLC
www.5foldmedia.com

For bulk orders of twenty (20) or more books, contact 5 Fold Media by email sales@5foldmedia.com or call 315-314-6480.

For reasons of confidentiality, the names of the author's friends, doctors, and nurses have been changed to protect their privacy; however, all the events shared in this book are as they actually occurred.

ISBN: 978-1-936578-55-9

Library of Congress Control Number: 2013931478

Dedication

I dedicate this book to my loving husband, Steve, who has been my greatest cheerleader, and to our sons, Samuel and Nathaniel, two of the greatest gifts God has given me on my journey towards wholeness.

Father,

I thank You for Your forgiveness
that is extended to me this day.

Show me Your ways today,
show me Your purposes.

~ Judy

Acknowledgments

I would like to thank the many people God has brought into my life who have been such an influence and encouragement as they helped me to see this book come into fruition:

To my "Sissy," who has been a rock for me; thank you for being my best friend in the whole world!

I want to sincerely thank my in-laws, Wes and Gloria, for all their love and support. They have been like second parents to me.

I also want to thank Randy and Janice Rupe for all their love, encouragement, and spiritual guidance as I went back and relived this painful time in my life.

To Pam McLaughlin, thank you for bringing order out of chaos as we worked our way through my journals and the manuscript. Thank you for encouraging me every step of the way.

Thank you, Dr. Larry Keefauver, for your insights and advice on the publication of the book.

I especially want to thank my Lord and Savior Jesus Christ for I know without Him I am nothing.

> *Now glory be to God! By his mighty power at work within us, he is able to accomplish infinitely more than we would ever dare to ask or hope. May he be given glory in the church and in Christ Jesus forever and ever through endless ages. Amen (Ephesians 3:20-21).*

Note From the Author About the Interactive and Small Group Discussion Questions Found in this Book:

Like most of us, I have found I have 20/20 hindsight. What I couldn't see at the time becomes painfully obvious as I look back. My prayer is that you will use these insights to carefully examine your own life and, if you see any similarities, get help before you get any further along this potentially dangerous path. As you read through and do these interactive exercises either by yourself or in a small group, I pray you will come to know our Heavenly Father as I did and find the help that will truly change your life from the inside out and that will move you forward on your own amazing journey toward wholeness.

Contents

Out of the depths have I cried to You, O Lord. Lord, hear my voice; let Your ears be attentive to the voice of my supplications. If You, Lord, should keep account of and treat [us according to our] sins, O Lord, who could stand? But there is forgiveness with You [just what man needs], that You may be reverently feared and worshiped. I wait for the Lord, I expectantly wait, and in His word do I hope. I am looking and waiting for the Lord more than watchmen for the morning, I say, more than watchmen for the morning. O Israel, hope in the Lord! For with the Lord there is mercy and loving-kindness, and with Him is plenteous redemption. And He will redeem Israel from all their iniquities (Psalm 130:1-8 AMP).

The Lord spoke to my heart tonight
that I really need to let the memories of my past live in me,
and only share them with those who might benefit from them.
~ Judy

Introduction: Looking Back

When I look back and try to recall the past, a wide variety of emotions begin to course through my mind. I'm embarrassed and ashamed, yet at the same time I am also amazed as I see how even when I was so far away from living a godly life, Jesus was always there holding me and waiting for me to turn my heart to Him. It seems an impossible task to try and express how much the Lord means to me and how thankful I am that, though I dropped to such depths of pain and despair, when I finally looked up, Jesus was there waiting to pull me out of the pit into His loving forgiving arms.

My prayer, as I strive to openly share all the painful memories of that disparaging chapter of my life, is that the Lord would guide me and work through my story to bring hope and healing to others who may be caught in the grips of this distorted self-image lifestyle as well as other self-destructive addictions.

I love Psalm 130:1-8 because it really captures the heart of where I was. I can truly say from the bottom of my heart that with the Lord there is mercy and loving-kindness, and with Him is plenteous redemption. He will redeem everyone who comes to Him no matter what their iniquities are. If He could love and forgive me, He can and will do the same for you!

Part One: Why Me?

I hate myself more every day.

But why?

I've got to find some answers soon!

I can't take it!

~ Judy

Chapter One: In the Beginning

I was brought up in a very close traditional Catholic family. In fact as I grew up I thought everyone was either Catholic or going to hell. My brother, two sisters, and I attended a Catholic school right up through high school. My mother was Italian and thrived on caring for her family. My father was an Irish Catholic hardworking man who had a hard upbringing. At the age of five, he saw his brother burn to death in front of him on Halloween night. He lost his father to cancer as a teen. He joined the U. S. Navy when he was fifteen. I knew my dad loved me and provided all of the physical needs like food and shelter, but he never gave me the demonstrative affection or verbal affirmation I longed for. As I look back, I see that I wanted to be special and noticed by him and I was never sure that I was.

We had this ritual we went through as we prepared to go to bed at night that might help you understand the type of relationship I had with my father. We would kiss my mother good-night then we would go over to where my father was sitting and we would kiss him on the cheek. Then he would extend his hand and we would each shake his hand. We thought that was totally normal. It wasn't until I became an adult that I realized just how impersonal my relationship with my father was.

However, my life felt warm and safe until it was time for me to enter kindergarten. My two older siblings were already in school so most of my daylight hours were spent with my mother, my younger sister, and my maternal grandmother who lived with us. The thought of leaving my mother for school every day was very threatening to me. From the day

I started kindergarten until I was in the fourth grade, I always wanted to run home from school as quickly as I could get out the door.

It got to the point that my anxiety would literally make me feel ill. Staying in school became a physical challenge for me. Today experts would call this separation anxiety, but at that time my teachers and parents thought that my symptoms were just ploys to get out of going to school. Realizing that the adults did not believe me and seeing the other children apparently adjusting to school, I began to think something was wrong with me.

It was not that I disliked learning. I actually excelled academically, consistently maintaining an "A" average. Everything seemed to come easily for me. Even though I hated being away from my mother, I found that bringing home good grades earned my parents' praise. This was not the case for my brother and younger sister. Even though they studied harder and longer than I did, my mother always told them she knew they could do better.

My older sister was twelve years older than me so instead of feeling the need to compete with her, I grew so close to her that she shared her feelings and struggles with me. As often happens with teenage girls, she began to draw away from our mother and closer to me. This made me feel even more special. The negative side to this though was that I learned about sex and drugs, and was exposed to things most girls have no knowledge of until much later in life. When my sister went away to college, I felt like I had lost my best friend. I entered a whole new phase of my every increasing need to please my mother and father.

Sibling Rivalry Births Competition

Once my older sister was basically out of the picture, it became a whole new playing field. My need to please began to develop into a very competitive approach to asserting my place in the family. I have since learned that in a family where there is ten years or more between the first and second child, a whole new birth order is established. Since there were ten years between my older sister and brother, I now became the middle child. I was two years younger than my brother and two years older than my younger sister. Some refer to this as the Avis or middle child syndrome. Whoever is in second place must try harder to effectively compete with the one in first place.

Discovering I could gain the praise of my parents by excelling in school set the pace for an intense desire to be better academically than my brother and younger sister. When my older sister went off to college, my increasing competitiveness saw this as a golden opportunity to get even closer to my mother. When my mother received a letter from my older sister saying she was pregnant, my relationship with my mother rapidly accelerated. Mom was horrified by my sister's letter and feeling she couldn't share it with my father, shared her shock and hurt with me instead. I tried to offer her comfort trying to be strong for her even though I really did not fully comprehend the situation.

From then on I tried to be the strong one in the family. I thrived on comments from friends and other family members telling me how together and levelheaded I was. I began to build an image that to the outside world showed I was strong and mature for my age. However, there was still a scared little girl hiding on the inside that required a lot of energy to keep hidden and controlled.

The Challenges of High School

I was able to maintain my new image until it was time to enter high school. I went from a class of twenty-two to a high school class of two hundred and twenty. Now there were two hundred and nineteen other kids to compete with academically. Though I had to work a lot harder in high school and was able to maintain a 90-95 overall average, there were always eighty or so other students that were at the same level. My competitive nature drove me to broaden my horizons. I had always been a good athlete in grammar school so I tried out for the volleyball team and made it. I played on the team for three years and did well.

My brother, sister, and I had all taken piano lessons. They hated it and decided to quit, but I saw this as an opportunity to excel in another area where my brother and sister could not. I found I really loved it and ended up taking piano lessons for eight years.

I started making some close friends in high school and deliberately chose those who were very smart, finding they actually helped me maintain the high academic average everyone had come to expect of me. Halfway through my junior year, I was well established in academics and sports, but found all my friends also had a very active social life. So I began to party and drink with my friends to expand in an area I thought was lacking in my life.

My parents never dreamed their little Judy would even think of doing such things so it wasn't too hard to maintain my image with my parents and my peers. As our junior prom appeared on the horizon, I found I was in need of a date. What I thought was just a date for the prom turned into a two-year relationship.

The Challenges of Dating

I thought Mitch was the best thing that ever happened to me. He was from a first generation Polish Catholic family. As a matter of fact, his parents could barely speak English and were very traditional and ethnic. Even though he was a year older than me and attended a different high school, my parents loved him. He already knew what he wanted to do with his life which impressed all of us.

He was in the R.O.T.C. program and wanted to major in political science in college as well as serve as an officer in the Army. He had decided to go to an out-of-state college but switched to a local college instead to be near me. I was preparing to go into a nursing program in the area. We were in love and basically spent every waking minute together.

The summer before my senior year, Mitch had to go away for his two-month basic training. We both agreed those were the loneliest two months of our lives and we didn't want to be away from each other like that ever again. So for Christmas he gave me a pre-engagement ring and we planned to marry in three years once we both finished college. I was so happy. My friends all told me how lucky I was. I had a guy who loved me, a future in nursing, and had proved to myself and my family I had a wide variety of talents. Everyone said I was gifted in art and poetry as well as music and had a great future ahead of me.

Your Turn

Our family of origin can shape and mold who we are and how we feel about ourselves. My family of origin was a mixed bag of love, shame, fear, and religion.

• How has your family of origin contributed to the strengths and weaknesses that make up the person you have become?

Read Romans 8:28.

> *And we know that God causes everything to work together for the good of those who love God and are called according to his purpose for them.*

Think It Through

Many people look at this verse and think that God thinks everything that happens to us is good. That's not the case. God is loving and kind and is not happy with the trauma, hurt, and neglect that some experience at the hand of their care-givers or family. He does say that He can use all those experiences for good. That is a big difference. He wants to reach down and meet us where we are and take us to a better place within ourselves. Won't you let Him use all your experiences, the good and the bad, to help you move forward to a more abundant and prosperous life?

Chapter Two: Anorexia–Chains of Affliction

After the excitement of the Christmas holidays and the announcement of my pre-engagement to Mitch, January brought with it a new calendar year and a whole new competitive challenge. Once I had made sure everyone knew about my pre-engagement, I found I had nothing else to compete in until I graduated and entered nursing school. I became very bored, but also anxious at the same time; separation anxiety was increasing concerning school and home.

I had worked hard all through high school at a local grocery store in customer service to help pay for my education. My job seemed so routine. School was no longer a challenge; the courses I was taking seemed very easy. I had even started taking some college courses offered in my high school to get a head start on college. I had my career plans, had already been accepted at the college of my choice, and was "pre-engaged." My relationship with Mitch also seemed to have slipped into a routine. I had nothing to compete in and nothing to put my energy into. I felt restless, unnoticed, and empty.

I didn't know it at the time, of course, but I was about to enter a three-year season in the "wilderness" where God would begin to reveal to me who I was and what I needed to see about myself so I could become the person He had destined me to be.

As I look back, I am reminded of what Moses told God's people about their wilderness time on their way to the Promised Land. "Remember how the Lord your God led you through the wilderness for forty years, humbling you and testing you *to prove your character*" (Deuteronomy 8:2, emphasis mine) . It wasn't God that needed to see what was in their hearts and what their character was like; He already knew. These people had to see what was buried deep in their own hearts and deal with it or they would never be able to live a victorious life, even in their Promised Land.

Entering My Wilderness Time

One of my closest friends had begun losing weight over the summer before our senior year. Up until January she hadn't really been very popular, but even over the Christmas holidays while everyone else gained weight, she continued to lose. There was such a noticeable difference that everybody began to praise her for her weight loss. Up until that point I had never really been concerned about my weight or thought of myself as overweight. However, when I realized how people noticed when someone had achieved obvious success in losing weight, I decided this would be my new challenge. I couldn't allow my best friend to get all the attention. The thought of this new arena of competition was just what I had been looking for to get energized and excited about life again.

I was 5'8" and weighed 143 pounds, so I saw no harm in losing a little weight. It had taken my best friend several months to lose the weight so I was determined to do it faster. I went right to work on this in January. I began to cut down my food intake and eating very healthy foods. In a few weeks I had lost eight pounds. I can't even describe the sense of achievement I felt. At first no one noticed, but as the weight came off the alarms came on and my mother became concerned. I reassured her I was fine and just taking off excess weight like some of my other family members.

My friend was 5'4" and had gotten her weight down to 115 pounds. By the beginning of March I had brought my weight down to 130 pounds. Even though my total weight loss surpassed hers, I was determined to weigh less than she did. I wanted to look thinner, and have the numbers on the scale prove I was thinner. My classmates began to notice my weight loss and started praising me for my willpower. So many girls my age were concerned about their weight and had tried but failed at dieting.

I had learned how to achieve success but I wasn't about to share it with anyone. I drastically cut my calorie intake to less than 500 calories a day and increased my physical exercise to an hour a day.

By May, my friends began to get concerned. There was a girl in our school who was one year younger than me that had a disease called anorexia. My friends pointed to her and told me if I kept dieting I would end up looking like her. When I saw how my friends looked at this girl with such concern and attention, I decided I wanted that same attention and concern from them as she was receiving. Seeing this as a new dimension of this challenge, I closed my eyes and asked God to allow me to be "anorexic" so I could achieve a unique thinness for a person my size. I didn't care what I would have to do.

Anorexia

Up until this point, I had never even heard of anorexia and wasted no time finding out all about it. In the months that followed, I read and found out everything I could about this condition. I wanted to know every method and trick that could be used to not only lose weight but lose it fast. I found that by taking diet pills, I could stop my hunger and taking diuretics helped me lose water weight. Boy, did the weight come off! I reached 115 pounds by graduation day and was still losing. People began to comment on how thin I had gotten and began to express their concern.

My parents did not say much so I thought they did not care. I could not believe I was losing all this weight and they didn't seem to notice. But when my mother did try to express her concern, I quickly changed the subject and became good at avoiding such conversations. I didn't want to hear it. I didn't want to stop, and I didn't want to admit that what I was doing was wrong. I loved the control. Even though my eating habits were strange and ritualized, I began to feel very clever in how I ate and kept control over my food. I ate the same food every day so I could be in control.

I don't need to say that this whole obsession affected my social life. I would still go to parties, but skipped eating for the day so I could drink and not have to worry about the calories. Mitch and I stopped going out to eat, and holidays and birthdays were days to be feared. There was a time when I began to realize how my dieting had started to take control of my life, but I just couldn't give it up and sacrifice my thinness. I had lived for so many months feeding my body on praise and control, that the thought of normal eating made me think of getting fat, being lonely, and just being average. In fact, at 115 pounds I still thought I was fat. As I look back, I can see what I was really dealing with here was a severely distorted self image.

Some good friends of the family, who came to my graduation, took my parents aside and expressed their concern over my weight loss and my obvious obsession with my weight. They explained to my parents about an eating disorder called anorexia that they thought I might have. My parents were not blind; they knew about the disease but had not been able to effectively approach me about their suspicions. However, hearing concern from so many people helped encourage my mother to take action.

The next day my mother took me aside to express her concern. She asked me if I thought I was anorexic. I was stunned that she even knew what it was, but of course I said, "No." She told me she thought I needed help and wanted to call my doctor and schedule a checkup. Actually, I was curious to see what the doctor would say so I agreed to go. I had the physical and afterwards the doctor had a consultation with my mother and me. He diagnosed me as having anorexia nervosa, a mental obsession with one's body image which results in compulsive dieting and rapid loss of 40-60% of one's body weight. I couldn't believe my ears. I did it, I really did it. I was anorexic. Now what? The doctor explained that this disease could be treated by seeing a child psychologist who specialized in this disease.

During all this I just thanked God for answering my prayer. I loved every minute of it. To think that I had this unique disease and would actually get to go to a psychiatrist made me feel I had achieved something close to impossible. Not many kids my age experienced that and the attention I was receiving, so I went. I met with this doctor twice before he confirmed that I indeed had anorexia. He proposed two ways of treating the illness. One would be as an outpatient and the other would be an inpatient treatment in the hospital. He asked me which one I preferred.

I hated the idea of both of them. After all, I had just spent six months trying to get to the point where I really had this disease. Now they wanted to take it away from me? Plus, it meant I had to gain some weight. I really just wanted to be left alone. I asked for a week to think it over and went camping with some friends. During this time my friends encouraged me to try the inpatient treatment feeling it might go faster and still allow me to enter college in the fall.

Mitch was away at basic training for the summer and was unaware of what was going on. I was experiencing the loneliness of being away from him again so I decided to try the in-hospital treatment. After all, I thought, there was nothing exciting to do over the summer but wait for Mitch. I called him and told him what the doctor had said. He was upset and agreed I should go to the hospital for treatment. I was admitted to the hospital two days later having lost even more weight. I was now at 108.

Your Turn

When life seems empty and purposeless, sometimes we look for something to fill that void, a new kind of "high" even though it may be destructive. For me, it was controlling my body image through my anorexia, which in turn became my new addiction, my new high.

• Life at times can feel futile and purposeless. During those times in your life, how have you tried to fill the voids?

Read Ecclesiastes 8:15.

> *So I recommend having fun, because there is nothing better for people to do in this world than to eat, drink, and enjoy life. That way they will experience some happiness along with all the hard work God gives them.*

Think It Through

Without God, life is meaningless and futile. When we seek to fill our lives with things that are out of the will of God, they can produce depression and hopelessness. A life with God is filled with tremendous purpose. You too can experience this God-fulfilled life. Won't you turn to Him to fill those voids in your life?

Chapter Three: Revolving Door

As I began what I thought would be my three-month treatment in the summer of 1983, my expectations of life in a hospital were quickly altered. I was placed on a floor with other psychiatric patients with various problems ranging from drug abuse, attempted suicide, various forms of depression, and a few others with eating disorders.

The first thing I learned was I had given away all forms of control over my life. All control was immediately taken away from me. They told me what I was to eat, how much to eat, and when. They decided how much weight I needed to gain. They even controlled when I could go to the bathroom, making sure I was supervised even then. I couldn't even leave the floor without a special pass and, of course, a staff member.

During this time I worked with a team of nurses, one of whom was a woman named Marie who became a very important influence in my life. At the time though, I saw the whole thing as a plot to take away every bit of control I had worked so hard to gain over my life. My doctor came three times a week and I had group therapy four times a week. I also started attending family therapy sessions once a week. They kept me busy, but I soon came to regret my decision to do the in-hospital treatment.

During this time I was exposed to some very frightening realities, and learned how many troubled people there are in the world. I also realized anorexia was not a disease one could get over in three months. It required a realization that what I had been doing was not only wrong, but self-destructive. I really wasn't there yet, so I also lacked the necessary desire to change. For the treatment program to work there needed to be a commitment and a will to overcome. I didn't have or want either. As a matter of fact, I actually learned more weight loss tricks from the other girls there with the same problem.

My mind was constantly being probed for information about my childhood and about each member of my family. I came to the conclusion that my family was to blame for my eating disorder. I developed a deep hatred for each and every one of them. My family grew apart and became very frustrated with me.

Inpatient to Outpatient

By August of 1983, I had gained the required weight my team and doctor had set for me. Feeling I had accomplished their goals, I began to lose weight again using some of the new tricks I'd learned from the other inpatients. I was actually thrilled that I had found some weight loss techniques my team wasn't aware of. I decided I wanted out. I wanted control of my life and my weight again. One afternoon I just walked off the ward and was gone all night. The police and my parents were alerted. I had no real plan other than to get away from there, so after spending the night wandering the streets, I eventually made my way back home.

By the time I arrived home, I was very upset and depressed. I convinced my parents that it was time I left the hospital and get on with my life. I assured them I could do much better on the outpatient treatment program. The police tracked me down and I had to return to the hospital. The program I was in required I be officially released from the program by my attending physician. The team I worked with and my doctor didn't agree I was ready to leave, but by this point I was not cooperating with my treatment, so they discharged me a week later.

I had started college while I was still in the hospital, but had already missed some of my classes because of the inpatient program. Once I became an outpatient, I moved into the dorms. I had only been out a week when I decided to stop seeing my doctor as well as my dietician.

My mind was made up to start losing weight again. I was now at 117 and back in control of my life, or so I thought.

As much as I wanted control of my life back, I found attending nursing school was very stressful for me. I had broken up with Mitch which added even more stress to the situation. I decided to focus my energies on not only losing all the weight I had been forced to gain in the hospital, but move my weight to an all time low. I began using diet pills and diuretics again as well as vomiting to lose weight.

Once I set my mind on this goal, I decided to quit school. I hated the program and I hated nursing, so I moved back home in November of 1983. My parents were aware I had not been doing well on the outpatient program, but I convinced them it was because I hated school and living away from them. I reassured them that by living at home I would be able to recover much better; I lied.

In the five months I lived at home, I worked a full time job at the same local grocery store I had worked at all through high school and had no social life or friends. It seemed everything had radically changed in my life those three months I was involved in the inpatient treatment program. Even though I thought leaving the hospital would allow me to regain control of my life, circumstances around me seemed beyond my capability to handle.

I was no longer pre-engaged; I was no longer in nursing school, and my relationship with my family had deteriorated to the point I hated the condition my life was in. All my friends had moved on with their lives while I was out of contact with them. Though I was back to losing weight, I had reached a point around Christmas where I was well on my way to severe depression. I had gotten my weight down to 105, but I still felt heavy and had not even come close to the goal I had set for myself.

At the same time, I couldn't stand how irrationally obsessed I was with my weight. I decided to go back to therapy and started seeing a woman therapist. She was very comforting, but I just couldn't find the desire within me to really get better. I felt I was wasting the money I had worked so hard for on something that was obviously not helping, so once again I stopped the therapy sessions.

By Easter of 1984, I was so physically ill that I couldn't even work a full day. I began taking days off on a regular basis. This added even more stress as the threat of losing my job constantly hung over my head. I remember going to Easter Mass with my family and hating every minute of it. I was so angry with God that when I got home, I ran to my room and silently screamed at Him for doing this to me. Physically and emotionally exhausted, I collapsed on my bed and just cried and cried. I cried about how terrible I was and how empty my life was. I cried because the control I so desperately wanted seemed way out of my reach.

As the list of negative things in my life grew and grew, I decided I really did need help. I began to realize—maybe for the first time ever—that I couldn't do this alone. Without even taking the time to wash the tears from my face, I sought the arms and support of my mother. When I told her I needed and wanted help, she cried and thanked the Lord for answering her prayers.

Your Turn

My destructive behavior cycle put me in the hospital where there were many people to help me. However, at this time in my life I was not ready to receive their help.

• In what ways have your destructive patterns of behavior and thinking kept you from receiving the help that has been made available to you?

Read Proverbs 14:1:

> *A wise woman builds her house; a foolish woman tears hers down with her own hands.*

Think It Through

Have you ever walked through a revolving door? You enter from the outside to exit into the inside. You are looking for a way out of the revolving door so you can get to where you need to be. In the same way our lives can get us caught up in vicious cycles that keep us running around in circles and not taking the obvious exits. Wisdom says I have been there before and I do not want to go back. There must come a time when you say, "I want out of here."

Foolishness will keep us running around in circles getting ourselves deeper and deeper in the depths of despair. There is a way out and God will show you if you are ready to take the necessary steps. Are you ready?

Chapter Four: A Glimmer of Hope

My mother took me to a doctor who specialized in eating disorders. At this point, I weighed in at 98 pounds. He gave me a week to gain at least one pound as proof that I would commit to working with him in an outpatient program. A week went by and I had lost four more pounds. It wasn't that I didn't want to get better, but I was so scared, so mentally obsessed, and so used to living this way that I didn't know how to eat normally or give up control. The doctor readmitted me to the inpatient program in April of 1984 for the second time in seven months.

The hospital was a bit reluctant to allow me to come back again after my last experience there. They weren't convinced I was serious about getting better. I had to meet with them first and share what had happened to me in the past seven months. After visually seeing my condition and talking with me, they had the proof they needed and agreed to readmit me.

I was so relieved and thankful to be back in the only safe place I knew. At that point I think I really began to understand how serious my problem was, and what a struggle I was having trying to overcome what I now saw was a destructive obsession. Although I never had a desire to get better before, this time was different. I was ready to do anything they asked of me. I needed to spend more time on redeveloping my eating habits, as well as try to repair a very abused and mistreated body. As I began this new phase in my treatment, much of my time was spent on gaining weight. I had more to gain this time. It was scary, but I knew I had to do it.

Dr. Fargo

During my second admission, I found myself in desperate need of a therapist. I wanted a private doctor and not one of the residents. Marie was still working on my team and suggested a doctor she felt would be good for me. I had called many others and had been declined many times because of busy schedules that I hesitated to call another. But she was so sure and confident that this doctor would say yes, and I was so desperate that I called. Sure enough, he said, "Yes."

Dr. Fargo and I were perfect for each other. We worked together very well, but more importantly I began to really listen to everything Marie had to say. After all, she had been right about Dr. Fargo. The time I spent with her talking and listening was a time of receiving encouragement and discipline. It was time I couldn't get enough of.

She seemed to know all about the inner turmoil I was in before I even expressed it—growing up, independence, change, and emptiness. When we would talk there was something about her I didn't understand. Something the other people didn't have. She had so much wisdom and insight, but most of all she had confidence in me. She really motivated me to start making some changes in my life. I decided I needed to learn how to be independent from my family and find out who I really was. I decided to move away from home. In order to do that I needed to find a job that would be able to support me as well as cover all my doctor bills.

My parents were devastated when they found out I was planning on doing this. They felt so strongly that this was a wrong decision that they offered no support as I moved forward with my plans. They also decided not to continue with family counseling sessions since they felt these sessions seemed to be tearing us further apart. In my mind it seemed they just weren't ready to let me go anymore than I was ready to let them go. However, I truly felt this was the first step in discovering who I really was deep down inside.

During my stay at the hospital, I had become very close with another girl staying there who also had an eating disorder, bulimia.[1] She was as determined as I was to get better and get on with our lives. We decided to look for an apartment together. We thought that besides decreasing

1. Bulimia is a serious eating disorder that occurs chiefly in females and is characterized by compulsive overeating usually followed by self-induced vomiting and is often accompanied by guilt and depression.

expenses, we could be a support to each other in our recoveries. We discussed with our teams the pros and cons of the situation and why we wanted to try, so our teams and doctors supported our decision.

After many months of searching and help from Marie and another nurse, we found an apartment. By this time I had a good paying job at one of the local hospitals as a heart monitor technician. The job required no experience but offered on-the-job training, and would definitely help me financially to move into this new phase of my journey toward recovery.

Discharge plans were made, and after a six month stay in the hospital, I was discharged. I had a new apartment, a new friend, a new job, and a new outlook on life. But what I wasn't aware of was I still carried the same "in look" about myself; that had never changed. I was like so many others who do not realize that until we deal with our inner self, we just carry our excess baggage with us from one location to another.

I had not yet come to the realization that we can change our outward environment, which may cause some beneficial change in our journey toward wholeness, but until we effectively change our hearts and minds, there is no real lasting success in overcoming whatever we have allowed to control our lives. Our battle begins within us.

I have since learned that there is really only one truly effective way to change ourselves from the inside out. I was about to get some insight as to what or rather *who* that was.

Introduced to Jesus

I didn't know Jesus then, but during my second admission I was certainly introduced to Him. As I look back at how God orchestrated things around me to help me see what the true solution to my problem really was, I remember a girl named Ann who was in the hospital the same time I was for an eating disorder. I really watched her because even then I could see there was definitely something different about her. For one thing, she was actually getting better.

I may not have had my head totally together at the time, but one thing I did know, if someone was really getting better I needed to find out what she was doing that I wasn't. I needed to know what she knew that I had obviously not yet discovered. I could also see that though we were both facing the same seemingly insurmountable obstacles, she faced them with peace while I hated every minute of the battle. As we became closer, she confided in me that she was "born again" and was trusting Jesus to heal her. I had absolutely no idea what she was talking about. That was definitely not what I expected or wanted to hear. As a matter of fact, I had to fight my first instinct to laugh in her face.

Though I didn't laugh outright at her, I didn't hide my anger at God as I countered with, "What do you mean God is healing you? He's the one that did this to you in the first place!"

Ann patiently answered my questions and listened to my doubts, and then she began to share things with me from God's Word. She showed me passages dealing with the body, food, self-image, and many of the other things I was dealing with. I tell you I just sat there and cried. I couldn't believe my problems were actually talked about in the Bible. Ann also told me that some of the people on her team at the hospital were also Christians. That's when I began to wonder if that's what was wrong (or right) with Marie. If she were a Christian, then that might explain why I felt so reassured around her. She, like Ann, had an assurance that I could not only overcome this disease, but move on and live a productive life.

I thought back to an incident that happened when Marie was helping me look for an apartment. One day she came across an ad in the paper and showed it to me. It said that two single young Christian girls were looking for a roommate. When I read that I was shocked that Marie would even consider that as a possibility for me.

I told her flat out, "There is no way I was going to live with a bunch of religious fanatics."

I see now how the Lord was preparing my heart to receive Him, even then. He was making Himself known to me through people like Marie and Ann. The only thing was I never thought I would need God when I was better and away from the hospital. Sure He answered the prayers of the sick, but what about when you are better? Besides, I had already decided that once I was out of the hospital and moved in my own apartment, I would be back in control, and there was no way I was ever going to let anyone, let alone God take that control away from me again.

Thank the Lord He knew me better than I knew myself. He knew the only way I would truly surrender to Him was to let me take over all control. The only way I would ever see just how much I needed Him was to try and make it on my own. I was going to learn this lesson the hard way. One thing I know though as I look back, He never left me and He never gave up on me.

Your Turn

I learned from my family of origin at an early age that God was someone to be feared. I needed to be a good girl to win His love and approval. Upon hearing different thoughts about God in the hospital from a patient and a nurse, I needed to challenge my initial belief system and open myself to something new.

• To what degree have you developed good relationships? What positive or negative effects have these relationships had on you? Have you begun to have a good relationship with Jesus?

____

____

____

____

Read Hebrews 11:1:

> *What is faith? It is the confident assurance that what we hope for is going to happen. It is the evidence of things we cannot yet see.*

Think It Through

Faith is a hard thing to explain. How do you explain putting trust in someone you cannot see? However, that is exactly what we are faced with as we begin to develop a relationship with Jesus. It requires faith that He is who He says He is, and that He can do what He says He will do. This was all new thinking for me. How about you? Are you ready to move toward trusting in Jesus and believing what the Bible says about Him?

____

____

____

Chapter Five: Flying Solo

Once I left the hospital, my roommate and I immediately moved into our apartment. It was great to be out of the hospital. I was healthy and facing a new life of independence away from my parents and the confines of inpatient therapy. My parents did not approve of my living away from home. They told me they were afraid I would become sick again. Their remarks just challenged me to prove them wrong, and to show them I could handle my life and any problems that would come up living away from them.

The sense of freedom that I felt living in my own apartment was nearly indescribable. Going to work and coming home to my own place, doing the grocery shopping, cooking my own meals, and even paying the bills gave me such a feeling of accomplishment. I was doing it; I was really doing it!

Even though I wasn't receiving inpatient treatment, I was still seeing Dr. Fargo once a week, and returning to the hospital for aftercare with my primary nurse. I had so many support systems in place around me one would wonder how I ended up back in the hospital for the third time. But I'm getting ahead of myself. For one brief moment, I felt I was in control and could do this on my own.

I worked the night shift at the hospital from eleven p.m. until seven a.m. which included weekends. My roommate worked from six in the morning until five at night and also worked weekends so we rarely saw each other. Though I loved being on my own, I was now faced with a lot of time all by myself. At first the rush of being in control was enough to keep me moving forward. But it didn't take long for the lack of friendship to allow all those inner fears and insecurities I had never really dealt with to rise to the surface again. More importantly, I realized how empty I was still feeling on the inside. I began drinking a lot and going out to bars to try and fill that void.

I also began hating my job. I was used to very active jobs so the hours of inactivity and sitting around all night just gave me more time to dwell on the confusion that was slowly creeping back into my thinking. All I could think of was all the weight I would gain by just sitting there and that definitely scared me. I tried to counteract these thoughts by running three to five miles each day right after I got home. That was one of the ways they had told me to get a handle on those fears of gaining weight. It is also said to help battle insomnia and depression. Even though I began to see the warning signs of backsliding, I felt I was doing the right things by running every day.

The problem was I also started weighing myself every day. At first that was a good thing because it confirmed I was not gaining weight. But when I saw my weight go up a little, I panicked. I immediately started cutting things out of my food intake to help control my weight. Then I stopped seeing my dietician because all I would do was lie to her about what I was or wasn't eating. It was then I realized that "it" was back again. The desire to be in control and to have something that would give me visual proof that I was getting results became my main focus. I needed something I could count on to fill the emptiness in my life, something that I could be successful at. I was feeling like such a failure that I was going back to something I was good at. I was good at losing weight.

I decided to quit my job at the hospital because of the hours, but mostly because of the overwhelming responsibility that was placed on my young shoulders. I was a cardiac heart monitor in charge of watching, recording, and measuring patient's cardio output from a twenty bank monitoring system. Every night there would be someone I had to watch more closely than the others, but I had to keep an eye on the others as well.

One night a woman I was watching went into heart failure. I alerted the nurse, and the doctors were there in minutes. Though I could not physically see this woman, I watched her die as the slip of paper coming out of the machine told me her heart was not responding to their efforts to revive her. I could tell she was dying. I wanted to go to her and help her, but that wasn't my job. I couldn't stand being so helpless. All the money in the world wasn't worth sitting there night after night watching people die, so I quit.

Nothing is Working

I went back to work at the grocery store working in general merchandise. I was making half of what I made at the hospital so it became harder to pay the bills. I had to cut my expenses somewhere so I told Dr. Fargo that I needed to look for a less expensive way of treatment. Although he tried to convince me we could arrange some kind of payment plan, I just didn't want to get into debt.

I can't even begin to explain with mere words what it was like for me to leave his office that day. Though I had convinced myself I was doing what I had to do, I felt like I was saying good-bye to the only person I could really trust. He was the one person that understood what I was going through and truly cared for me even when I was doing badly. I cried for weeks.

I entered into such a state of depression that I couldn't pull myself out of it. I decided to go into therapy with my primary nurse, Samantha. She had worked with me at the hospital and was actively involved in the eating disorder support groups in the area. She was starting a private practice of her own so my sessions with her were less expensive than with Dr. Fargo. I found that my insurance did cover some of it so I felt I could do the sessions and still keep my head above water financially.

However, talking with Samantha was nowhere near as effective as my sessions had been with Dr. Fargo, but she fulfilled the need I had to have someone to talk to. I missed Dr. Fargo and began comparing her methods with his. Samantha was not as compassionate as he had been, and seemed more interested in my mother than she was in me.

I was also attending the support group for girls and women with eating disorders once a week, but it seemed all we did was sit around and talk about how bad everyone was doing. If anyone was doing well, it seemed to me the only evidence was they had gained weight. I began associating getting better with getting fatter, so I stopped going to the support group as well.

To top off my downward spiral, my roommate and I were having major conflicts in our relationship as well. She was always on my back to keep eating and not to give up, but she seemed to be having just as many problems as I was overcoming her own eating disorder. I began to feel very threatened by her. My competitiveness began to take control so my new goal in life was to be thinner than she was. I began hating her for preaching to me about getting better when she wasn't getting any better either. I felt so defeated; nothing was working. Doesn't anyone ever get better?

I started eating less and even started vomiting what little I did eat. The cycle started all over again. My weight started dropping, but I hated being around my roommate because she knew what I was doing. Where it had been easy to hide it from my parents, I couldn't hide it from her. We talked and cried a lot. I decided it would be better to give up the apartment and move back home. She decided to do the same. I dreaded telling my parents I wanted to move back home, but I knew that was my only option; nothing else was working.

Moving Home

I felt so defeated and like a failure when I told my parents I wanted to come home. To my surprise they were very supportive and told me that their house would always be my home. My roommate and I wanted to spend Thanksgiving together in the apartment. I did not want to go home on a major eating holiday and deal with all the stress I was feeling. I realized how very sick I really was when holidays that I had once enjoyed became days I wanted to forget. It was a very lonely day which ended up in a fight between me and my roommate.

My vision of overcoming this disease had been shattered in less than ten weeks. As the full impact at what I had done began to hit me, I tried to read the Bible but nothing made sense—nothing touched my heart. I tried to sleep but to no avail so I decided to restock all of my diet aids prior to going back home. As I went down the aisles of the drug store, I came across the sleeping pills. I looked longingly at them thinking the only peace in my life right now was when I was asleep. However, tonight that even seemed to elude me. I went back to the apartment, took some sleeping pills, and started to pack. I was really hoping I could fall asleep and stop thinking about all that was wrong with my life.

Three days later, in November of 1984, I moved home and right back into my old room. Everything was exactly as I remembered it. As I stood there looking around at the walls, I realized I hated that room. It reminded me of all the terrible things I had thought about and done to myself, so I decided to paint it. I thought if I painted it a bright color, yellow perhaps, it would somehow cover the darkness I was feeling inside. I was still trying to control things on the outside without really changing anything on the inside. I was still running away instead of dealing with the cause of my problems. Once again though, when I packed my bags to move back home, I brought all the old baggage and even more pieces had been added to it.

I had not yet learned that it is not what I eat that brings real joy and peace into my life.

Your Turn

My life was beginning to feel like a series of false starts. Relationships, jobs, and anorexia left me hopeless and in despair again. I shunned the support systems that were put in place for me and as a result, nothing changed in me or my circumstances. I was eager to be on my own and prove to everyone that I could handle my life myself, that I did not need anyone. The result was complete failure, and more and more depression and hopelessness.

• What kind of community do you desire around you so you are not flying solo and heading for failure?

____

____

____

____

Read Ecclesiastes 4:9-10:

> *Two people can accomplish more than twice as much as one; they get a better return for their labor. If one person falls, the other can reach out and help. But people who are alone when they fall are in real trouble.*

Think It Through

In this verse God tells us we do not have to go it alone. In fact it is wiser to have someone around to help and support you. How foolish is the one that thinks they can go it alone. They are destined to be stuck with no way out. Don't you want to get out of where you are? God is waiting and willing to be that one to walk with you through this valley in your life.

____

____

____

Your Story

Take this opportunity to write down what you have discovered about yourself up to this point in the book.

Today's Date: ______________________

My family of origin: ______________________

Empty times in my life:

Destructive behaviors and thought patterns I have identified:

My current feelings about a relationship with God:

The kind of community I have around me now, and the kind I desire to have around me for success:

Part Two: Where Do I Go From Here?

I met some really nice people
who I think can help me out of this!
I just wish I wanted to be helped;
the thing is I don't yet.
~ Judy

Chapter Six: Can Anybody Hear Me?

I was home alone painting one day when loneliness and fear of the future completely overwhelmed me. It was just too much to bear. It seemed no matter what I did, I couldn't get away from the constant barrage of negative thoughts. As I kept reaching for something to grab onto, a name flashed across my mind, Barbara.

Yes, I thought, *I need to talk to Barbara.*

She was a patient I had met in the hospital who had given me a Bible. Though she was no longer taking the inpatient treatment, she kept in touch with me while I was in the hospital the second time. I hadn't heard from her in a while though and I wondered why her name had suddenly come to my remembrance. I remembered she had talked about how God had helped her overcome her own self-destructive behavior. The last time I had spoken to her she told me she felt I needed God as well. Desperate to talk with someone who had actually overcome her self-destructive lifestyle, I prayed to God that if He really loved me He would have Barbara get in touch with me again. Though I wasn't sure God even heard my prayer, I did feel a little better thinking I had done something positive for a change.

I was truly surprised when a half an hour later the phone rang and it was Barbara saying she knew I was in trouble. I was blown away that what I had just uttered as a prayer had come to fruition. This was pivotal for me. God showed up and I knew it was His doing because I had prayed. God had my attention now! When I asked Barbara how she could possibly know that I was in trouble and needed her to call, she said God had put my name on her heart. I really wasn't sure what that meant but since I had prayed and she had called, I figured God must have had a way to communicate with her. She asked me how things were going and I told her I was out of the hospital, but definitely not cured. She quietly listened to me and then said she felt more than ever that God had the answers that I sought. She explained to me how she felt God had helped her and what He could do for me.

She always sounded like she had a close relationship with God and could talk to Him about anything. I thought to myself how wonderful that must be so I asked her to send me some literature to help me learn how to have a relationship with God like she did. I also asked her to see if she could find me a priest or church leader that I could talk to about my situation. When I hung up I was so thankful she had called. I was eager to get the literature she had promised to send me. Having something to look forward to definitely made a difference in my attitude. I began to think maybe God was watching over me after all.

He Knew My Thoughts

It didn't take long though for my mood to turn dark again. I was only home two days when my mother realized I wasn't eating and that I was losing weight again. I could always sense when she was zeroing in on me and I wondered why I had even tried to come home again. I could feel the hatred begin to rise up within me again against everyone around me, especially my mother. One night when I didn't eat dinner with my family, she came into my room and began yelling at me. I couldn't believe it when she sat down on the edge of the bed and started crying.

"How could you do this to me and your father?" she screamed.

Caught totally off guard, I screamed right back at her, "What do you mean do this to you? What about me? What about how I feel?"

Though I was angry and hurt, I caught a glimpse of what I had done to my family and especially to my mother. I saw the sadness and the fear and the hurt in her face, and I hated myself even more than I hated everyone else.

I had to leave and go somewhere where I couldn't hurt anyone anymore. I ran out of the house and drove away with no idea where I was going or what I was going to do. I decided to go to a movie thinking I might find an escape from all the hurt, at least for a few hours, by sitting alone in a darkened movie theater. The next day was even worse. Another dinner I didn't eat with the family and another argument with my mother convinced me I couldn't live there no matter how broke I was. I was beginning to think there was only one way to rid myself of this disease which was tearing my world and everyone in it apart—kill myself.

As I drove toward the highway formulating the easiest way to end my own life, I passed by my older sister's house. I was crying so hard I could hardly see the road so I thought maybe I should try talking to her. I had tried everyone else; maybe she could help me. I talked, she listened. I finally told her I didn't know what else to do, I just wanted to die. I wanted to kill myself so I would stop hurting everyone around me. She told me how foolish that was and said she would help me find other options. She started by calling Samantha, my therapist, and told her what was going on. Samantha and I talked for quite a while. Every so often Samantha would ask me again if I was going to hurt myself.

I couldn't promise her or anyone that I wouldn't. I just didn't know what to do. I felt like I was drowning with no hope of ever being rescued. Samantha told me she thought it would be best for me to be readmitted to the hospital for a while until they could help me deal with what she called "my severe depression."

Although the thought of going back into the hospital for the third time made me feel like a failure, I knew in my heart that it was the only safe place for me to be. I knew it was a place where people were concerned about me, and wanted to help me. Samantha made the arrangements and my sister went back home with me to get some of my things. I was relieved to find my mother was not at home, but thought how ironic it was when my father told me she had gone to an anorexia support group meeting for parents.

As I was packing, I saw all the diet and sleeping pills I had bought just before I moved back home. Without even thinking twice about it, I started taking them one-by-one. I'd throw a piece of clothing into my bag and then take another pill. By the time I was packed, the pills were gone. I went downstairs to tell my father I was going back into the hospital. He was sitting at the kitchen table doing the books for his store as he did every night. I put my suitcase down and he looked at me questioningly. I told him that I needed to check myself into the hospital again because I didn't trust myself right now. As I was trying to explain how I was having thoughts of hurting myself, my father suddenly pulled me into his arms and cried as though his heart would break.

I had never in my life seen my father cry. I don't think it was until that moment that he realized how much I was hurting and how sad I had become. It was also the first time I realized how he was feeling and how helpless he felt. I had broken his heart and had failed him. I had made my father cry. He told me that he would tell my mother what was going on and that he hoped this time I would really work to get better.

There it was again. Just when I thought somebody in my family might actually understand what I was going through, they let me know they thought all I had to do was try harder and I'd get better. We sat in silence as my sister drove me to the hospital. She dropped me off at the entrance and as I walked to the desk to admit myself I thought, *Here we go again.*

As I sat there scared and alone waiting for someone from the floor to come and get me, I looked up and saw Marie coming toward me. What a sight for sore eyes she was! She greeted me with such warmth and concern that I knew I had made the right decision. This was definitely where I needed to be.

She put her arm around me and said, "You look awful. Have you eaten today? Come on, let's get you settled in, get you some food, and then you can tell me what has been going on with you."

This was one of those experiences I now refer to as "a God intervention." I didn't learn until later just how pivotal this particular God intervention was for me.

Your Turn

Being home again was adding misery to both my life and that of each of my family members as well. They watched me cycle back to my old destructive ways. I thought a change of location and a fresh coat of paint would make a difference, but it didn't. I was still the same on the inside. In desperation I cried out to God and asked Him to send help through a phone call from one of my friends. To my surprise the phone call came almost instantly. Was God really hearing the cries of my messed up self?

• Have you ever cried out to God wondering if He could hear you? What were the results? How did that affect your view of God?

____

____

____

Read Psalm 139:4:

> *For there is not a word in my tongue (still unuttered), but, behold, O Lord, You know it altogether. (AMP)*

Think It Through

This verse tells us that even before we speak, God knows what we are going to say. That day when I cried out to God to have my Christian friend call me, I was floored when she did. But that is the kind of God we can have a relationship with—One who knows our every thought even before we speak it. That day I began to see that maybe God did understand me after all. Can you believe that God has that same care for you and your situation?

____

____

____

Chapter Seven: Secure At Last?

I distinctly remember thanking God for allowing me to be back in the hospital and for letting Marie be there right when I needed her. That night Marie and I talked for quite a while. I talked about what I was feeling. She made me eat something and then put me to bed. She knew I was feeling like hurting myself so she ensured my safety by removing all potentially dangerous objects from my room. I didn't trust myself in the state of mind I was in, but I realized God obviously knew where I was and this was where I needed to be at this precarious time in my life.

I lay in bed, glad I was safe and among people who cared for me, but even happier to be near Marie again. I had such trust in her that I vowed that night to listen to everything she had to say. Though I felt safe, I could not sleep. The pills I had taken made me feel sick. The longer I laid there the more I feared the morning. I feared walking down the hall and having to face all the staff that I had worked with before. I feared having them ask me why I was back in again. It was a long restless night and the next morning I found my fears were totally unfounded. The staff members on the floor were great. They understood what I was going through and were all glad I had sense enough to realize I needed help.

Although Samantha had been my outpatient therapist, she couldn't be my inpatient therapist because she was still working as a nurse on the floor. I had a choice of working with a hospital resident or finding another private doctor. I was so sick of trying to find a doctor, especially having to start all over again with someone who didn't know me or anything about me that I decided to just meet with a resident. It didn't take long to realize he didn't know the first thing about anorexia or about my past history. He and I did not get along well at all. As we concluded our very first meeting, he told me he felt I could probably leave in a week or so. He thought if I were put on an antidepressant that it would solve everything. I think my jaw must have dropped to the floor. I couldn't believe this doctor thought that by giving me a pill I could get better in a week. I wondered if he even heard me tell him that I had previously been in the hospital for ten months and even that had not been long enough.

I talked to Samantha and told her my concerns, but she too felt a short stay was all I needed. They both seemed to think that by medically dealing with my depression, I could go back out into the world and handle all the everyday challenges and pressures of life. I decided to talk with Marie about it and she told me she felt I had a lot to work out and that it would take some time. She encouraged me to contact Dr. Fargo and ask him if he would consider taking me as his patient again. Fear gripped me at the thought of calling him. What if he said no? I was so afraid of rejection that I put her off and told her I would have to think about it.

The first week back was a very confusing and lonely time for me. I didn't have a doctor I could really work with. Here I was contemplating suicide and I had some resident asking me about my childhood and telling me all I needed to do was take an antidepressant and I would be just fine. *Who cared what happened fifteen years ago?* I thought. *Why couldn't he see I was hurting now and needed someone to care and give me direction—now, today?*

Marie assumed the role of my primary nurse, as Samantha prepared to leave the hospital to pursue a career in private practice. Though I didn't realize it at the time, this was another answer to prayer. Though I was grateful to have Marie, I became more depressed and hopeless as that week went on. I wanted so much to work with Dr. Fargo, but I was afraid to ask for his help. I was at the point that even one more rejection could push me over the edge for good.

Thoughts of hurting myself still occupied my every waking moment. I began searching for a way to hurt myself, but as strange as it seems, I didn't want it to be too obvious. I somehow thought if they really cared about me they would notice I needed to be rescued even if it looked like I was trying to hide it. I had begun smoking a year prior to this, and one day as I sat lighting a cigarette and trying to think of a way to physically hurt myself, I held my lighter up in front of me and just stared at the flame. I wondered what it would feel like to hold against my skin.

I took my lighter and laid the flame against the back of my right hand and counted. I wanted to see how long I could hold it there before the pain got so bad I had to move it. I did this repeatedly, trying to increase the length of time. I felt pain but at the same time it almost felt good for a change. I was so sick of feeling emotional pain that the physical pain seemed to overshadow it.

Plus, physical pain was something I could control. I wanted a permanent scar on the outside that would reflect all the pain I was feeling on the inside. A scar would be a constant reminder to me and to everyone else of the pain I was feeling on the inside. I don't have to tell you that the burned flesh on my hand was the ugliest thing I had ever seen. As I looked at my blackened skin, I felt this was a very accurate description of what I thought I looked like on the inside. I was very satisfied with the way it looked, feeling I had achieved what I had set out to do.

It wasn't long before a nurse I worked with noticed the nasty looking burn on my hand. When she attempted to question me about it, I had nothing to say. She knew the way I had been feeling and how destructive my thoughts had been so she called the resident doctor to come and look at it. He immediately put me on the fire precaution's list and on a suicide watch. But this didn't stop me. I found another lighter and was at it again. I was amazed at how much pain I could endure. I was fascinated by the reaction of my skin to the flame.

Marie became concerned when I seemed to be getting worse instead of better. So one night she sent the burn resident to come and look at it and check for infection. I loved the attention and was anxious to find out how much damage I had caused so I didn't put up any fight. They told me it was a third degree burn which might need a skin graft, but I would still be left with a permanent scar. After the resident left, I silently shouted, "Success at last—a permanent scar!" I wanted a visible scar to represent all the pain and hurt I was feeling on the inside and now I had one.

Marie realized what I was really doing and talked with me about why I did this to myself. She told me I had to stop acting out my feelings but rather to put them into words. She told me to find a way to express all the feelings and emotions I was keeping bottled up inside with words. She patiently explained I could achieve the same results with written words if I would just tap into what would turn out to be a talent I had not yet discovered I possessed.

She also encouraged me again to call Dr. Fargo. She reminded me that I didn't have to hurt myself for Dr. Fargo to care about me. He had already proven that to me. I admitted she was right and with much fear and doubt, I called him. I talked to him for a long time and he agreed to work with me again on the grounds that I would continue with him when it was time for the outpatient treatment. I agreed.

I can't adequately express the relief and joy I felt to have my doctor back—the only one who really knew me inside and out. He was the one who truly cared for me no matter what I did or said. Finally, I had something positive to look forward to. Now that I had taken the step to connect with Dr. Fargo again, I was eager to begin working on my problems. I really thought I was on the way back up from the deep dark pit I had fallen into. I had Dr. Fargo and Marie; who else did I need?

Your Turn

Being back in the hospital for the third time might sound depressing but considering the circumstances, that was the safest place I could be. God had worked out all the details. My nurse and my doctor were there for me, what else did I need? I believed that I was on my way out of my pit of despair, but I was really feeling a false sense of security. I had still not come to the place where I was willing to do what was needed to truly crawl out of the hole that I was in.

- What place or people do you run to that create a sense of security for you when you are still in that place of pain? Is it a place of false security?

Read Psalm 139:5:

> *You have beset me and shut me in—behind and before, and You have laid Your hand upon me. (AMP)*

Think It Through

This verse talks about the protection of God that surrounds us even if we are still trying to figure Him out. He protected me and had me exactly where He wanted me. He is always nearby, ready and able to show Himself as our protector. I know I needed one; how about you? Have you come to a place where you know you need to trust and go to God for your protection? Can you see evidence of His protection over your life?

Chapter Eight: Giving It All

It was only a couple of weeks before Christmas and here I was, still in the hospital. I had not really seen a lot of progress in overcoming my depression and my disease, but Marie and I had become even closer. We would sit and talk about my life, and its many problems. She would share that what I was going through— the loneliness and the emptiness—were things she too faced and had learned to walk through. She said if I didn't learn to walk through these things now, I would have to face them again and again until I did. Until I decided to face these challenges and work through each one, I could never move forward with my life. It would be like riding one of those horses on a merry-go-round. You could get on and ride it but when you got off you were still in the same place. Nothing had changed. I knew she was right but I had yet to figure out how to do it.

They had a piano at the hospital that I could play any time I wanted to. Sometimes sitting down and practicing what I had learned when I was just a child gave me some peace. I had forgotten how much I enjoyed the eight years of piano lessons I had taken as a child. As I practiced, the gift I had inside once again rose to the surface. One night Marie heard me playing and told me she had a song for me to try. She told me she would make a photo copy on her break and bring it to me. I was in bed asleep when she dropped it off, but when I discovered it the next morning and read through the words of the song, I started to cry. It was a song about me and my life.

As I read the words of the song, I realized I did feel "pleasure" from the anorexia and I was afraid to let it go. The song gave me hope as I read about a higher power that would hold me in the palm of His hand. It suddenly dawned on me that this "higher power" the song was referring to was God. It was like the writer of the song had been where I was and discovered God had been there loving and holding him all along. The rest of the words became a thank you prayer that I have sung many times since then.

At my lowest point, when I thought no one cared, there was someone, a higher power, who knew and understood my pain better than I did—God. I was overjoyed as I finally realized what made Marie different from everyone else; she must know God just like Barbara did.

That opened the door for me to talk about God with Marie. When Marie saw my response to that first song, she brought me a book of songs that were all about God. My love for music and playing those songs really began to minister to me. Hope began to fill my heart as I played and read the words to these songs about God and His love. I couldn't understand the Bible right then, but oh, how the music touched me deep down inside where I needed it most. I was to find out very soon why God had sent Marie and these songs into my life, but for now they provided a place of escape from the stress and pain.

God not only knew the gift of music that had lain dormant in my heart, He also knew there were a lot of other gifts I had never explored buried deep within me. He began marking where each gift was buried with an "X" even I couldn't miss. I was soon to discover how to dig for buried treasure and use my gifts to bless others at the same time. God knew the gifts I already had within me and used them to begin to work on my heart from the inside out.

Hidden Gifts

As the Christmas holidays approached, my relationship with my family became even more strained. My mother could not accept that I needed to be in the hospital. My younger sister wanted nothing to do with me. Each contact with them revolved around the fact that I needed to toughen up and come home. The holidays were coming and my parents impressed upon me how much they wanted and expected me to be well enough to come home.

I tried to explain my fears and why I didn't feel safe there. I knew it would be too easy for me to hurt myself at home. It seemed interaction with my family always created a desire within me to show them my inner pain through an outward physically destructive behavior. They never seemed to understand my pain and I couldn't seem to communicate it to them no matter what I said or did. This inability to convey my inner turmoil to my family always fueled my anger and pushed my self-destruct button. This was definitely not the way I wanted or needed to spend the holidays.

I did, however, want to give them all a gift. I had no job and therefore no money with which to buy presents. I decided to lean on my creative abilities and focus my energies on making gifts for everyone on my list. I made sweaters for my younger sister, my nieces, and my nephew. There were carefully crafted homemade ornaments for my parents and for my older sister. I came up with these gift ideas relatively easily, but I couldn't think of anything for my brother.

One thing I knew about my brother was he had a real hard time showing that he cared. He visited me a few times with his girlfriend and always made me laugh. I saw him start to take charge of his life in a way I wish I could. I looked up to him and loved him, but I had never really told him that. I had already started writing poems which was a way I found to express some of my inner emotions as Marie had suggested. Most of them centered on what I was going through at the time, but it helped me see how powerful written words could be.

I discovered I had the ability to express myself with words so I decided to write a poem for my brother. I asked God to help me write a very special poem for my brother that would show him how much I loved and admired him. I knew God answered my prayer as the words just seemed to flow from my pen to the paper, beautifully conveying a love for my brother I had never before been able to outwardly express.

Christmas Eve was very lonely on the floor. Most of the patients had gone home for the holidays and Marie was off for a few days as well. Though the excitement of making the gifts for everyone and anticipating their reaction to what I had made gave me a boost, this was not the way I really wanted to spend Christmas Eve. I felt very alone. The major holiday I had been anxiously preparing for was finally here and I was once again sitting alone in a hospital room seemingly no closer to overcoming my disease. I felt very depressed by my lack of success and began to think how great it would be to die on Christmas. My parents would then have a constant reminder of just how sick their daughter really was. I lost sight of what Christmas meant and focused only on myself.

I may have felt all alone and that no one knew I was sitting alone in a hospital room on Christmas Eve, but now I know God knew right where I was and exactly what I needed right then. He sent Terry, a male nurse who worked on my team to check on me. When he saw my unhappiness, he sat and talked with me all night. I shared with him my thoughts about dying and he shared his concern for me. He told me he cared what happened to me and that I was a very special person. He said that he would miss me if I died, especially my sense of humor. I had to laugh at that. I needed to hear that people cared about me and that not everything about me was as bad as I thought.

The Greatest Gift

Christmas Day came. I didn't attend services at the hospital; it just didn't seem the same. Even though it had been my choice to stay at the hospital instead of spending Christmas at home, I missed being a part of the family traditions. I was still feeling sorry for myself when my parents, sister and brother arrived with many presents for me. But even the presents didn't help to change my dark mood. Nothing they could give me could make me happy. But as I gave each of them what I had made for them and watched their expressions as they opened their gifts, I began to feel something stirring inside of me.

I watched as tears fell from my parents' eyes. I had taken so much time with each gift and even my sister didn't try to stop the tears as she looked in amazement at what I had made. They knew these were things that didn't come from a store, but from my heart. I handed Jim the poem which was mounted on a piece of stained wood with the paper outlined in the form of a tree. He read it, and then looked up at me with tears rolling down his face. When He got up, came over and hugged me, you could have heard a pin drop; the room was so quiet.

Everyone was totally surprised by his emotional response. None of us had ever seen this side of him. My heart rejoiced as I realized the words from my heart had broken through his tough exterior and touched his heart. I knew I hadn't written that poem by myself. God had used the gift He had placed in me to touch my brother's heart. I suddenly realized this was what Christmas was really all about—giving of one's self to build up another.

After my family left I realized that this was exactly what God had done by sending His Son to earth on Christmas Day. Jesus was a gift from God's heart to us and for us, specifically designed for each of us—just like the gifts for my family had been specially made by me. I didn't yet fully understand why God had given us this gift or what I needed to do to truly receive it for myself, but I knew God wanted me to know the real reason for the season.

I was still experiencing confusion, doubt, and indecision about what needed to be changed in my life, but God knew all about me and was preparing me to receive His ultimate gift. I received the literature from Barbara a few days after Christmas and she called to see how I was doing. She began calling me even more frequently and telling me she was praying for me. She encouraged me to read the literature she had sent and ask her any questions I had about it. She told me that she believed the Lord had His hand on my life right then.

In a way I knew that was true, but the same old questions kept coming back to haunt me. How could a loving God allow me to be so sick? Why wasn't He listening to my cries? It would take a few more acts of desperation before I would realize God had indeed heard my questions and knew how to answer them so I would never have to ask them again.

Jim (Christmas 1984)

This year don't look beneath the tree
For the gift I give you, you will not see

No box to unwrap, no bow to untie
So look with your heart and not with your eye

Please listen carefully so as not to miss
A life long warranty on your Christmas gift

I give to you more than some gifts can say
A gift that keeps giving every single day

Your gift comes in parts—can't say it's easy to use
But in time with some practice it will if you choose

The first part I give are my ears for to hear
Your every trouble your every joy when others aren't near

The second part that I give is my eyes for to peer
For those times when confusion makes your vision unclear

The third part that I give is my thoughts and my dreams
For those times when it's easier to dream on a team

I also give my hands to touch
When others around seem only to clutch

Even when you're angry don't put my gifts away
It's at those hard times they can help calm your day

But my most important gift is my last gift to you
It's the part you can't be without no matter what you do
For it's that first part I give not just this first year
But it's that gift I promise giving when we no longer are near

It is my gift of love for you that originates in the last part
It's the only gift I wrapped for you, it is wrapped within my heart

Your Turn

Being in the hospital during the Christmas season limited my ability to come up with gifts to give to my family. I had hurt them so much during the past year that I longed to bless each of them with something special. I used the talents that I had within me to reach out to each of them, not knowing that God was sending me a gift that would change my life.

• How has your destructive lifestyle or thoughts interfered with your ability to share yourself with the people closest to you?

____

____

____

• Are there some talents that you have allowed to remain dormant that you should be using to help others?

____

____

____

Read Luke 6:38:

> *If you give, you will receive. Your gift will return to you in full measure, pressed down, shaken together to make room for more, and running over. Whatever measure you use in giving—large or small—it will be used to measure what is given back to you.*

Think It Through

This verse does not talk so much about what we give, but the attitude with which we give. We are encouraged to hold nothing back, but to give it all. That is the way the Father has given to us—by sending His Son on Christmas to be the Savior of the world. Jesus was the greatest gift ever given to mankind, wrapped in human flesh, and given to all. Have you heard about this gift? Have you accepted God's gift?

____

____

____

Your Story

Take this opportunity to write down what you have discovered about yourself up to this point in the book.
Today's Date: ____________________

No matter where I am or what is happening in my life, I am never alone because:

The difference between true security and false security:

My destructive lifestyle or thoughts have interfered with my ability to:

These are gifts and talents I have discovered within me:

God has given me His greatest gift:

Judy Roberts at a 1983 family birthday party.

Judy Roberts with younger sister three months after first hospitalization. The dog, Dooley, was a gift to help her take care of something as well as herself. She had already begun to lose weight again.

Judy Roberts in April of 1984. Drastic weight lost had led to a second hospitalization. This was the day she was admitted.

Judy Roberts weighing the least she had in two years.

Part Three: What Do I Do Now?

I want to find out who Judy really is
and what she's about.
I've been this person nineteen years
and I feel I know nothing.
I don't know what she really wants.
~ Judy

Chapter Nine: Heaven or Hell?

Barbara called me one day at the hospital and said she had found a pastor for me to talk to who had worked with girls with eating disorders. I really thought that was strange that a man of God knew about this disease. The only contact I had with the church was when my Catholic priest visited me in the hospital, but he only wanted to talk about the weather and make jokes about hospital food. He never asked me about what I was going through although I would try to talk to him about some of my problems. He didn't seem to know anything about eating disorders or even why I was in the hospital. He never said anything about God helping me solve my problems or that God would be able to help me get better.

I told Barbara I didn't think I was ready to talk with this pastor, but I promised to let her know when I was. I tucked the option away in my heart just in case there came a time when I had run out of other options. I wasn't aware of it right then but this was all part of God's plan to bring me to a place where I would run out of ways to do things my way. Then I would have to turn to the only One who could truly bring about lasting change in my life.

Happy New Year?

It was January, a new year and I was still fighting myself every step of the way. On the one hand I had vowed to do whatever Marie suggested, but on the other hand was my fear of giving up control. I believed everything Marie said I needed to do to overcome this disease was true, but I just didn't seem to be able to let go and give in. I still wanted to be thin, and I knew that getting better meant giving up control and gaining weight. I knew that by giving up control I would have to face the emptiness inside my heart and I just couldn't do it, not yet. The funny thing was that fear was really the thing that was in control, not me.

I would try to tell myself I couldn't go on living like this. I'd remind myself of how many times I had already been in and out of the hospital and how each time I left I was risking my health. But before I could convince myself it was safer for me to face my fear of change than to go on like this, my anger would kick in and I would silently scream, "Why do I have to live this way? Why doesn't anyone even try to understand the constant battle I am having with my will?"

Everyone, even Dr. Fargo and Marie, made it sound so easy—you either want to get better or you don't want to get better. As I looked at my image in the mirror I thought, my problem goes even deeper than that. I wanted to want to get better. What I really needed was someone to help me figure out how to let go of the thin, sick Judy and take hold of—just Judy. But who was this Judy? Did I even want to be her?

Still struggling with the confusion and anger caused by all these unanswered questions, I went home on a one-day pass to pick up my car and bring it back to the hospital. I had decided that to even move forward just a little I had to start thinking about the future. As a small first step, I wanted to start the new year by having my car at the hospital. I knew I was going to need to find a job and that would be difficult without a car. I was actually quite proud of myself for even being able to think of looking for a job.

However, when I got home I found my youngest sister had been using my car while I was in the hospital. She angrily accused me of being selfish by taking my car back to the hospital, knowing I would be leaving her without a car. I couldn't believe how upset she was and how she seemed much more concerned about the car than me. Once again I realized my sickness and what I needed to do to get better was an inconvenience for my family. Why should I even try to get better?

I was so angry and hurt that when I went to my old room for a few more things and found a bottle of anti-depressants and a bottle of muscle relaxers, I grabbed them both and threw them angrily in my bag. I got into my car without a backward glance and spun the wheels in my need to get away from there. As I drove back to the hospital, my thoughts were totally consumed by just one thing. I was going to stop this cycle once and for all. I had what I needed to kill myself now, but I needed to watch and wait for just the right time.

My parents came up to the hospital that night and I got into another argument with my mother. She told me again how she felt I was running away from my problems by coming and staying in the hospital. My father agreed with her saying I was using living at the hospital as a crutch. I couldn't believe what I was hearing. What did they mean I was running away from my problems by participating in the inpatient therapy program? I was here because I was trying to deal with my disease. I was here trying to face my fears and my problems head on.

I was so angry with their obvious lack of understanding, I started crying. I knew I was on the verge of hysteria so I asked them to leave and quickly headed back to the sanctuary of my room. *Why did every visit with my parents turn into such a disaster?* I contemplated as thoughts of ending my life once again took center stage in my mind. By the time I got back to my room, I knew exactly what I was going to do. I took all the pills I had brought from home.

As I sat on my bed waiting for them to take effect, I thought of what would happen if I died tonight. All I could see ahead of me was peace—peace at last. There were no parents, no sisters, no hospitals or doctors, and no food in this peaceful place I was heading for. But then a terrifying thought suddenly occurred to me as I remembered reading a question in the literature Barbara had sent to me, "Do you know where you are going when you die?"

Where will I go when I die? I wondered as panic began to replace the peace I thought I was heading for. *Is it possible I could go to hell?*

Surely God could see I had no other choice and that there was just no other way out, right?

I began to really panic as I realized I wasn't sure where I would go if I took my own life. I couldn't chance it, not yet. I prayed to God right then and there and asked Him to spare me and to not let me die until I knew for sure where I would spend eternity. I can't tell you how scared I was.

I tried to throw up the pills, but couldn't do it. *Now that was a first*, I thought. Now what? I had to tell Marie what I had done, but I was afraid if I did the hospital would make me leave, then where would I be? At this point, the fear of death and an unknown eternity took over so I ran to find Marie. I told her I needed to talk to her right away. As soon as we got in her office, I started crying hysterically. As shame at what I had done began to overwhelm me, I nearly changed my mind about telling her but knew if anyone could help me it was Marie. I thought she would yell at me when I told her, but she didn't. She was more concerned about how many pills I had taken. Once we figured out about how many I had ingested, she called Dr. Fargo.

I don't remember much after that; I must have passed out. I seem to remember bits and pieces of the next couple of days. Later Marie told me what the doctors did for me that night. If I hadn't told Marie what I had done when I did, I might have actually accomplished what I had intended to do. I lost two days of my life, but did not succeed in ending my life. When I finally woke up and looked around, there was a nurse sitting next to my bed. My first thought was thank you God, I'm still alive. At that moment I didn't care about anything except the fact that I was still breathing and had a chance to make things right. In a flash of clarity, I realized God had answered my desperate prayer.

I asked the doctor not to tell my parents because I knew they wouldn't understand. I knew they would blame the hospital and probably take me out of there. I couldn't risk that. These people had saved my life; it was me who tried to end it. My doctor and Marie knew I wanted and needed to stay in the hospital. They did a lot of interceding on my behalf with the heads of the hospital to assure them that nothing like this would happen again and that I really needed to be there. I again thanked God for allowing me to stay in the hospital and get the kind of help I really needed. I knew it was time to start moving forward.

Your Turn

Desperation, despair, and discouragement added with anger and all that was happening in my life made for a terrible mix. Thoughts of suicide had entered my thoughts before, but this was different. I was tired of it all—the anorexia, the family, the hospital, and me. After taking the pills to end my life, it was my fear of where I would go after I died that consumed me and resulted in my desperate prayer to God that actually saved my life, just in the nick of time.

• If you were to suddenly die today where do you think you would go and why?

____

____

____

Read Psalm 146:5-6:

> *But happy are those who have the God of Israel as their helper, whose hope is in the Lord their God. He is the one who made heaven and earth, the sea, and everything in them. He is the one who keeps every promise forever.*

Think It Through

We can look for help in so many places and in so many people, but this verse says there is only One that we can really trust, God. We are to put our hope in Him because of who He is—the overseer of everything, including us. God is faithful and He will be faithful to you. You can know where you will go after you die; He has the answer. Are you willing to listen?

____

____

____

Chapter Ten: Second Chances

The following weeks proved to me and to the staff at the hospital that I had truly turned the corner. I started taking some definitive steps forward starting with my diet. Marie spent a lot of time with me on this saying she wanted to help me get my eating under control first. She assured me she wouldn't let me get fat, promising she would show me how to eat and exercise properly to maintain a healthy weight. She did so much more than just tell me what to do; she was in this with me and I knew it. She was as excited and eager as I was to see me move forward with my life, but she knew me well enough to understand the fears I would be facing. She brought me recipes that we would cook and eat together. We had been through so much together that I trusted Marie even more than the dietician that had been assigned to me by the hospital.

Marie kept her word on the exercise end of my training as well. She told me that she had personally found that running was a good form of exercise. She knew I was going to have to balance my eating habits with a sensible regular exercise routine. I began eating the way Marie suggested and running three times a week by myself which was another big step for me. I always hated doing things by myself, but Marie explained that this was another step I had to take in order to really overcome the fears that had gained control in my life.

I realized Marie was right. I needed to condition myself to overcome each fear so I could face the long road to recovery and stay focused even when Marie wasn't there right beside me. We both knew that there would come a day when I would have to have the strength to go it alone. With Marie's help, I started with running solo three times a week. Marie told me how to focus my thoughts and put my heart into running. I needed to exercise sensibly, motivated by a desire to get—and stay—healthy. After a while she began running with me, and we could both see my life taking a definite turn for the better.

As I moved into a healthy exercise and eating routine, the next thing we needed to discuss was what I would do once I left the hospital. I knew I needed a new job, but not just any job. I needed a job with direction. Most kids my age were in their second year of college and already knew what they wanted to do with their lives. I was in the hospital trying to fight a very destructive disease. I was also trying to find out who Judy really was and what she was supposed to be doing with her life. Choosing a career had not really been a concern for me up to this point. A job had merely been a way to earn money so I could be on my own and pay my bills. Now I was seriously thinking about what it was this new Judy really wanted to do with herself once she left the hospital.

One weekend Marie brought me a brochure from a local vocational school which offered courses in cooperation with local schools and colleges. She thought if I could find a short-term training program in something I really liked, it would help motivate me to move forward in this area of my life as well. We looked through the listings until we found a dental assistant's course that started in February, ended in June, and met only two nights a week. Marie and I discussed the possibility of attending the course even while I was still in the hospital.

It sounded perfect. I could meet my inpatient obligations and still attend classes. The only problem was that the tuition was $500, which might as well have been $5000. I just didn't have it and didn't know where to get it quickly enough to register for this class. It was the middle of January and there were only a few weeks before the class was to begin. Seeing my obvious frustration with the money issue, Marie offered to talk to the social worker to see what the possibilities were for the vocational training center to fund the money.

Finally, I had a direction, a hope, and something to shoot for. I thought that working in a dental office with other people around, and making good money sounded like the perfect job for me! I told my parents the news and they were pleased that I wanted to go back to school. Even they noticed my change of mood and attitude toward life. They seemed as anxious as I was to hear if I would get the necessary funding. A week later Marie took me aside and told me the funding had been denied. I was devastated. I sat there and cried as self-pity once again moved in and tried to take over my thoughts.

"How could they do this to me?" I screamed in anger. "Don't they understand how important this is to me?"

Instead of letting me wallow in self pity, Marie let me have it with both barrels, "If you want something bad enough, you need to go after it. You need to realize that anything worthwhile in life requires work. Why should you get upset when what you want isn't just handed to you? You need to stop whining and complaining; get back up, brush yourself off, and go after it."

Well, I did not want to hear that, especially from her! How could she be so cold? My anger focused on her. I felt it was her fault for building my hopes up in something she knew I couldn't get. I felt the hatred rise up in me toward her and stormed off to my room, deciding I wasn't going to listen to her anymore. I was sick and tired of trying. I was sick of having to work so hard for everything I wanted and needed in life. What did she mean by that comment anyway? Hadn't I been working hard to overcome my sickness? Was it my fault I was sick? Was it my fault I was in a hospital? Why was the world so cruel?

Your Turn

Up and down, up and down seemed to be the way I was going with my emotions and my recovery. I would make the hard decision to give in and work with my team, and then my hopes would be dashed, again and again. This cycle of disappointment just created more questions for me and I was ready to throw in the towel once again.

• How do you handle the cycles of hope and disappointment that can happen in your life?

Read Psalm 51:12:

> *Restore to me the joy of Your salvation and uphold me a willing spirit.*

Think It Through

Joy is an expensive commodity in this world. Once you have it, it can easily slip away if it is based on our circumstances and those circumstances change. The kind of joy this verse is talking about is the joy that comes from knowing the saving power of God in our lives. God has a plan to rescue us from our despair, but we need to be willing to ask Him. We need to be willing to continue walking out our life with Him—no matter what comes our way. God never changes and His ability to save us never changes. Do you want the saving power of God and the joy that it brings? Begin by asking God to grant you a willing spirit.

Chapter Eleven: Great News on a Napkin!

Shortly after this I decided to stop eating. I was trying to punish Marie for the whole vocational school thing. One evening I found myself in the dayroom sitting at a table across from Bob, a therapy aide who was on my team. Bob looked like a linebacker. He was a big no-nonsense guy and whenever I got assigned to him, I hated it. I sat there ignoring him and complaining to another patient about how the vocational school thing wasn't going to work out.

I was already in a foul mood when Bob started this annoying tapping on the table, I looked over at him intent on showing him just what a waste of time I thought this evening was. He was not even looking at me. He had his arms folded crossed over his massive chest and appeared to be watching something on the TV. He casually looked over at me and without even unfolding his arms, he pointed his index finger upward and looked upward. I looked up and then looked back at him with a *what the heck are you looking at?* shrug of my shoulders.

He pointed up again and looked up towards the ceiling again. He unfolded his arms, took a napkin from the center of the table and drew a picture on it like he was doodling. As I watched him, curious now as to what he was trying to communicate to me, I saw what looked like two cliffs with a big space in between them. He had my attention now because it looked liked something I had seen before. He drew a stick figure of a person on one cliff and he wrote the word "God" on the other side. Then he started drawing arrows coming off the stick figure going down into a pit between the two cliffs. He wrote things like weight, being good enough, and being smart enough around these arrows. At the bottom of the pit he wrote the word "hell."

I couldn't take my eyes off the napkin as he continued his simple, almost childlike drawing. He drew a cross across the gap between the two cliffs like it was a bridge. Finally, he drew an arrow of the stick person walking over to the other side where God was and then he drew the stick figure on the other side.

It couldn't have taken more than a couple of minutes for him to draw the picture. He was kind of covering it up with his body so nobody but me could see it. After he was done, he pushed it to me, sat back, folded his arms again and pointed up. Then he turned his attention back to the TV as if to ignore me once again. That was it. I took the napkin and stuck it in my pocket and forgot all about it.

I refused to eat or do anything for the next couple of days out of spite. Then one night, physically and emotionally spent, I lay on the floor of my room looking up at the ceiling. I was angry at everyone and everything. After all I had done and accomplished in a month, nothing had really changed. Here I was again, right back where I started but now I felt like an even bigger failure. I had really thought I had a chance to make it this time.

I cried out to God, "Why? Why all this pain and emptiness? Why are You doing this to me? I've tried everything—the hospital, the therapists, family counseling, and support groups. Is this all the world has to offer me for all my work, nothing? Is this what being low is? Can I even get any lower?"

I carried on telling God how much I hated being fat and hated living like this. Once I ran out of complaints and excuses, I opened the Bible that I had left on the stand next to the bed. I saw where I had left off with my reading. It was a psalm that talked about how God had created the heavens and the earth and everything in it (see Psalm 146:6). I was going to keep reading but my eyes and my mind got stuck on that word "everything." It just sort of stood out like a bright light does on a restaurant sign as you suddenly realize how hungry you are. I started to laugh. That's it! I finally get it!

I looked up again but this time my thoughts went passed the ceiling in my room; I needed to talk to the Creator, "You made everything, God. I believe that. So You know how everything works, which means You must know all about anorexia. You knew about it before I even knew it existed. And if You know about it, then you must know how to get rid of it."

At last something spoke to my heart. It had been so long since I had opened the Bible Barbara had given me. It always seemed hard to understand. I could never really see how it applied to me and what I was experiencing in my life. But this time it was different; it actually made sense to me. I knew right then and there that God must be the way out of the despair and pain in my life. I knew it. I had finally found the way to beat this thing that had plagued me for so long and had virtually paralyzed my life. But even as I began to think there was hope for me, doubt once again raised its ugly head. Was it really that easy? I had to be sure.

As I lay on the floor with my Bible open in front of me, I asked God to give me three days to prove to myself that my old way wasn't the way. I made a vow to God that if after three days I was still the same, then I would try things His way. Although I knew my way of dealing with life by starving myself was destructive and bad, I still needed to be able to really let go of it. I needed to prove to myself once and for all that my way only made me miserable. So for the next three days, two of which Marie was off, I stopped eating.

No one was aware of it at first, but it didn't take long for the nurses I was working with to be concerned that I might be digressing back into my old patterns. They kept telling me to not give up, that I had really been making some progress, and that starving myself wasn't going to change anything. I felt like telling them this is a test—only a test. However, I knew this was between me and God and that they would never understand why I had to do this one last thing.

My doctor was aware of what was going on and once he realized I wasn't letting up, he came in to talk to me. He told me he wanted to help but that he could not allow me to starve myself. He told me he wouldn't force me to eat at this hospital, but if I didn't start eating again he would send me to a place where he could.

Obviously I was jeopardizing my stay at the hospital so I reassured Dr. Fargo that I would begin to eat again. The things he shared with me just proved to me how much he really did care about me and how hard he was trying to reach out to me. If only I could just receive the help he was offering me, but I knew I had to take this first step on my own. I had to know I could trust God to give me the guidance I needed and to make sure I was on the right path before I could really surrender to doing things His way.

Your Turn

A napkin! Of all things that God could use to reveal His rescue plan to me, He used a napkin. What Bob drew showed me where I was in life and how I was separated from God by my own sin. I was on one side and God was on the other side. All of my attempts at reaching the other side fell short and always landed me back in the same situation. The cross of Christ was what Bob drew to bridge the two sides together. Was Jesus the way to the Father? Would He accept me? I wasn't ready yet to find out.

•In the diagram below where would you draw yourself?

___

___

___

___

Read Romans 6:23:

> *For the wages of sin is death, but the free gift of God is eternal life through Christ Jesus our Lord.*

Think It Through

The good news is that we do not have to be separated from God by our sin and misery. He has created a way to join Him and be in relationship with Him. It is through Jesus Christ, His Son. Do you want to take that step of faith to the other side? Keep reading!

Chapter Twelve: Oh Happy Day!

Alone in my room at night, I pulled out the information Barbara had sent me about how God works in us and through us if we would only accept Him into our lives and hearts. *Would He come—even into a messed up life and heart like mine?* I thought, *I had done so many bad things. Was there really hope for someone like me?* As I read further it was if God had heard my questions and was answering each one.

First it said God knows we are all sinners and without Him in our lives we are all a mess. Then it told me that if we acknowledge the fact that we have messed up and need God to not only fix us but forgive us, He will. All we need to do is ask Him into our hearts and He promises He will come. I was amazed at how simple God made it—admit it, confess it, receive it. I learned that God literally cleans us up from the inside out and restores us, but that is not all. He shows us a different way to live, a different way to go—His way. If we ask Him to take control of our present situation and our whole lives, He will teach us how to do things His way—the right way.

There's the catch, I thought. I had to really think deeply about the "giving Him control part." When it came down to it, though, what did I have to lose? I knew I couldn't continue the way I was going. I had to let go of my self-destructive ways once and for all and hold onto God with both hands.

Could I do it? I wondered. Could I really let go of everything and take hold of God with both hands?

The Horns of Dilemma

I went to my Bible and read every Scripture the pamphlets talked about. As I contemplated what God was trying to show me, I remembered something I had drawn months ago for Dr. Fargo after I tried to commit suicide. This was one of the assignments he had given me to do.

He had told me I was "on the horns of a dilemma." I told him I had no idea what he was talking about so he asked me to spend that weekend drawing what I thought my life looked like at the time. I still had that picture.

When I pulled it out I was amazed at what I had drawn. There were two cliffs that were connected by a rope bridge. I was standing on the left side and the part of the bridge closest to my side was frayed and very treacherous looking. The closer it got to the opposite side the stronger the bridge looked. I had this woman with me who was dressed in a multicolored suit. She was my "tour guide" and was pointing back toward the world behind me. She would not take me to the other side because it was too treacherous. As a matter of fact there was a sign right before the rope bridge that said, "Tour ends here." Across on the other side of the rope bridge I had made this big sunburst out of tissue paper, but I had drawn a big cloud blocking it so I could not see it from where I was standing. I had drawn a big telescope in my hands that I was using to try and see what was across the bridge.

I had told Dr. Fargo that I was trying to decide if I wanted to go across the bridge on my own. I realized I would have to put the telescope down in order to maneuver across the bridge. The telescope represented my anorexia. It was the lens I was looking at my life through. I had labeled my drawing, "Horns of Dilemma."

As I thought about the drawing I had done, I remembered the stick figures Bob had drawn on the napkin shortly after my suicide attempt. I was amazed at how similar the two drawings were. God was using them to help me understand that I was the only one that could decide what my next step would be. I had to decide if I would surrender everything, including my "telescope" to Him, and let Him guide me across the bridge He had made for me—the Cross. I began to understand the significance of the cross. Jesus had made a way for me to be forgiven and to walk into the arms of my loving Heavenly Father. It all started to make sense.

I Surrender

That night in February of 1985, I invited Jesus into my heart and life. I prayed to God confessing the sin in my life—all the areas where I had disappointed Him and missed the mark, and I asked Him to forgive me. I cried all night long because I knew He must be the way across the bridge and the answer to all I had been searching for my whole life. Even though my faith was so very small, I believed He loved me and cared about me. I looked back at the past three years and saw how He had allowed me to make my own choices and allowed things to happen to me as a result of those choices. I actually received just what I asked for and then when I got so low there was nothing left to do but look up, there He was, waiting for me to reach out to Him. He never gave up on me!

I told God that night that I was tired of trying to do things my way. I surrendered everything to Him.

I told Him, "I give up all control; it's in Your hands now."

I was truly at my lowest point and I acknowledged I needed Him—not the doctors, nurses or hospitals—just Him. He made everything, He knew how everything worked, and therefore He was the only one who could fix what was wrong with me and with my life. The pieces started falling into place. At last a peace surrounded me—a peace like I had never known. I can't even begin to explain how it felt when the weight of all that I had carried with me for so many years was literally lifted off my shoulders. That night I went to bed feeling the thinnest and lightest I had ever felt.

Your Turn

I could get no lower in my cycle of destruction. Attempted suicide, multiple hospital visits, deteriorating health, disappointment, and hopelessness were weighing me down so low the only place I could look was up. When I did, there He was! God had been there all the time, working out the details to bring me to the end of myself. I just needed to reach up and receive Jesus as my Lord and Savior, and hand the steering wheel of my life over to Him. I was finally free!

• How about you, are you ready to hand the steering wheel of your life over to Jesus as your Savior and Lord, receive His forgiveness, and allow Him to direct and show you God's way for your life?

____

____

____

____

Read Romans 3:23-24 and John 3:16:

> *For all have sinned; all fall short of God's glorious standard. Yet now God in his gracious kindness declares us not guilty. He has done this through Christ Jesus, who has freed us by taking away our sins.*
>
> *For God so loved the world that he gave his only Son, so that everyone who believes in him will not perish but have eternal life.*

Think It Through

If you want this relationship with God that is talked about in the above verses, then pray this prayer:

Lord, I admit that I am sinner and that I have done things that are displeasing to You. I ask for forgiveness and ask You to come into my heart, take the steering wheel of my life, and bring Your Holy Spirit to guide and direct me. I thank You for sending Your Son, Jesus, to die on the cross for me and take my punishment upon Himself. I gratefully await (look forward to) the days ahead of getting to know You more personally. Amen.

Chapter Thirteen: Step-By-Step

It was amazing how my life changed after that day, not all at once of course, but slowly and steadily. Day by day I began to change, but this time it was from the inside out. I began by searching and reading through the Bible every day. What used to seem like a foreign language to me now began to make wonderful exciting sense. So much of what I read seemed to apply to my life and the things I was struggling with. I was amazed to find all of the answers to my inner turmoil were right there in God's Word. How could I have missed it all these years?

I finally told Marie I was trusting God with my sickness and my future. That really opened the door for us to use God's therapy and not the world's version. We knew I had to start moving forward. I was determined to take the vocational training school course—still feeling that would meet my needs in so many different ways. Marie encouraged me to go to the Lord with my need; after all He was in control now, not me. *Well*, I thought to myself, *if God can pull this off then He must be real.* So I prayed and asked the Lord to provide a way for me to take this course and get the money I needed to pay the tuition. A few days later when I was talking to my parents and telling them my plans for the future, they agreed to loan me the money to take the course. That was my first direct answer to prayer. It proved to me that God was really taking control and that I could trust Him to provide what I needed so I could do what He was telling me to do.

I enrolled in the course and began attending night classes. What a difference it was to be out of the hospital at night and working toward my future. I felt like a human being again. The class was very small, and no one knew I was living at a hospital. I couldn't wait for the class to be over so I could rejoin the working world. I was definitely moving forward—step-by-step with God leading the way.

It seemed I was on the go from morning until night—meeting with my doctor, going to group and family therapy sessions, talking with my dietician, attending night classes twice a week, exercising, and talking with Marie about my future. I got back kind of late after class but Marie always made time for me. I felt very motivated and filled with great peace now that God was in the driver's seat of my life.

I began to have a deep desire to know God more. I wanted direction on what I was supposed to be doing if God was in control of every area of my life. This was all so new to me and I wondered what my next step should be. Once again I thought of Barbara. I called her and told her about accepting Jesus as my Lord and Savior. She was thrilled that I was now one of the Lord's own. I told her I needed to learn more about God and how to have a closer relationship with Him. I asked her if she would get in touch with the pastor she had told me about before. Might he be willing to come and talk with me about the things of the Lord?

She told me he had just moved to the area with his family and that he was starting a church near me. He agreed to come and see me at the hospital. The day before I was scheduled to meet with him, I went to the Lord in prayer. I told God I needed a church to belong to. I wanted a place where I would be among people who shared my love for God. I prayed for a small church, one in which maybe someday I would be able to share my love for music. I left the rest in His hands and waited for Him to show me what He had for me.

Pastor Brown

The next day there was a knock on the door of my room and when I answered it, there stood a man who introduced himself as Pastor Brown. I took one look at him and knew he was the one God had sent to me. He began by sharing some things about himself, his family and his relationship with God. I told him about my situation and the things I was facing at the time. He asked me about my relationship with God and

I explained how I had recently given my heart to the Lord. I was afraid he might not know what I meant, but of course he did.

Not only did he know what I meant, he wanted to open up the Scriptures to me even more. He went through Scripture after Scripture showing me what it meant to have Jesus in my heart. He brought me to a Scripture where Jesus was talking with a man named Nicodemus about having God living in us. Jesus referred to it as being "born again" (see John 3:1-16).

Pastor Brown showed me where Jesus explained about being born of the flesh and what it meant to be born of the spirit and why we needed that as well. He also explained what it meant to really surrender all to God—all we have and all that we are, and why we need to admit we are sinners. When he explained our need for a savior and why we need to confess with our mouths and believe it in our hearts, I began to understand how important what I had done was to my life here on earth as well as to my eternal life after I leave this earth (see Romans 10:9-11).

At first I had trouble grasping all that Pastor Brown was saying but it finally began to make sense to me. I realized that my past belief in God was just that, a belief that He existed. What I had failed to understand was that God is not someone we believe in and honor one day a week and then return to living our sinful life the next six days. I also realized that God didn't cater to or belong to a certain religion. God was someone we were to have a daily relationship with and not a weekly religion with. We were to have a relationship with God where we allow Him to be Lord of our lives every single day. That means what He wants for us, either in our behavior or the way we chose to live our lives should take precedence over our own personal desires. I saw such a change in my love for God and in my attitude about sin in my life. I literally felt as though I truly was "born again."

Pastor Brown visited me regularly at the hospital, sometimes two or three times a week. He brought workbooks for new believers that helped me with reading and understanding the Scriptures and finding out how to walk more closely with the Lord. Through these studies I found out that my walk with the Lord was a two-way street. Just because I had surrendered my life to the Lord didn't mean that I just sat back and waited for God to make things better in my life. As I read and studied the Scriptures, God began to speak to me through His Word about things that I needed to release if I really wanted to walk closely with Him and truly wanted His will for my life.

I discovered it meant that my obsessions with food and my weight would be the first things to go. I also had to eventually let go of the hospital and thinking that I always had a place to go when things got really bad in my life. The Lord showed me that He was the one I was to go to for everything. That was hard for me to hear.

Marie talked with me about these issues as well and helped me understand how important it was to be obedient to the commands of the Lord. She told me that in order for me to have the Lord work with me on the healing from this sickness, I needed to stop trying to control the situation. I needed to yield all my fears about what to eat, what not to eat, how fat I thought I looked, and even what the scales said I weighed—to the Lord. These were things I still struggled to hold onto. I constantly questioned Marie as to why God wouldn't just heal me quickly so I didn't have to deal with all of this.

Between Pastor Brown and Marie, I learned how important it was to learn how to do things God's way even if I didn't understand it at the time.

God's Way

Marie asked me something during this time that I will never forget: "What if the Lord healed you when you wanted and did it all at once? Would you still look to Him for everything, or would you think that your healing was everything you needed and continue to take control of the rest of your life instead of relying on the Lord?"

She told me that was not the way God did things. She said she believed God was going to use this disease and my healing from it to guide me and to keep me in line with His plan for me so I would not go back to my plan for me. Through the healing process, God would teach me to trust Him and see how faithful He was when I chose to obey and follow His plan. Marie knew how hard this would be for me, but she also knew that it was God's way of rebuilding an already weak vessel into one that could be used for His work.

I listened and I obeyed. I didn't do it perfectly and I spent a lot of nights crying out to the Lord for some sort of compromise of control. Marie helped me realize that trying to get God to agree with me wasn't the way things worked with my loving Heavenly Father. God wanted me to love Him so much that I would willingly obey Him and trust Him with my life. I learned that obeying and trusting were ways I could show I knew God loved me and that I loved Him, too.

School was going great and so were my sessions with Dr. Fargo. Although I knew the reason for my sudden change in attitude was due to my new relationship with God, I tried not to talk about it with my doctor. Though he was a caring and wonderful doctor, I knew he would never understand the "God" approach to my healing. God continued to use Dr. Fargo to show me how to achieve my healing, but I knew it was God that was helping me to be able to do what needed to be done.

While I was still in the hospital I began developing a closer relationship with Pastor Brown and his family. I also started to attend his new church which was not at all what I expected. It was completely different from the traditional forms of worship I had been accustomed to. The people were friendly and kind and eager to offer support to me. There were no man-made rituals, but rather an honest and open worship of the Lord. I was amazed to see that the traditional missals were not used in this church. Instead they actually used the Word of God, the Bible. The music and personal testimonies were uplifting, always giving me a feeling of family every time I was there.

I never really shared the reason for my new zest for life with my family during this time. Truthfully, I did not know how they would react. I was afraid they would be angry and non-supportive so I waited and trusted the Lord to show me when and how to tell them of my newfound relationship with Him.

My doctor was extremely pleased with my progress as he saw my self-destructiveness slowly melt away that he and Marie began to discuss discharge plans with me. I had always hated that word "discharge" because in the past it meant leaving for a short while until the disease took over again and forced me to be readmitted. However, I knew that this time was different. Though I was afraid, I really had a desire to leave and I was totally committed to getting better. I also knew that this time I had God helping and guiding me every step of the way.

I was told by many people that the recovery rate was only about five percent and that seventy-five percent of those diagnosed with this disease had reoccurring problems even while remaining on an outpatient treatment program. I was determined to be in that five percentile success group. This time I wanted to get out and live, but not for me, for a God who had opened up a brand new world before me.

Your Turn

A change came over my life almost instantaneously after I gave God the steering wheel of my life. Internally I was ready to gain the weight that I needed. I had a hunger for the Word of God and the things of God. My eyes were open now to all the people and situations that God had orchestrated on my behalf over the last three years. I was ready to get moving in the things of God.

If you are ready to start your walk with God, tell someone close to you the decision that you have made.

Read Matthew 6:33:

> *But seek (aim at and strive after) first of all His kingdom and His righteousness (His way of doing and being right), and then all these things taken together will be given you besides. (AMP)*

Think It Through

This verse challenges us to put God first in and above all things in our lives; and when we do, the promise is that everything else we need, like food, clothing, housing, and jobs will be given to us. He is a good Father and loves to bless His children; but more importantly, He is looking for us to develop a lasting relationship with Him. Can you think of ways to maintain your relationship with God? (Hint: How do you maintain earthly relationships?)

Your Story

Take this opportunity to write down what you have discovered about yourself up to this point in the book.

Today's Date ________________________

If I were to suddenly die today I know I would go to:

My joy in life comes from:

Things that cause me despair:

My relationship with God is:

Things I am afraid to give God control over:

Things I need to find out how God wants me to handle:

My prayer for today:

Part Four: Way To Go!

Waiting and thinking, looking for happiness.
No one said it would be easy.
This is the hardest thing I'll ever do!
(so they keep telling me)
Another day; one step closer.
~ Judy

Chapter Fourteen: Stepping Out

With a discharge date set for April 24, 1985, I knew I needed to find a job that would hold me over until I had completed my dental course. Marie told me to pray about it and ask the Lord to show me the job He would have me do.

It was springtime and I felt so alive. I wanted to do something different, something fun. I wanted to use my hands. I had always wanted to have a summer job working in a florist shop or nursery, and I thought again of this desire that had been hidden deep inside of me. I brought my need before the Lord and asked Him to either open or close the doors as I checked out each job possibility. I was learning that giving God control didn't mean I couldn't ask Him for what I thought I wanted. It simply meant I had to be willing to give up my idea if God said, "No."

I was also learning that God expected us to do our part and not just sit back and wait for Him to make things happen. I was driving to a local store to fill out an application when a sign along the side of the road caught my attention. I turned around to check it out more closely, and found it was a help wanted sign for an interior landscaping company. I wondered if this could be what I had been looking for. Disregarding my previous plans, I decided to inquire about the position.

I talked with a woman who said they had a temporary full-time summer position as an interior plant technician that could possibly lead to a permanent position in the fall. No prior experience was necessary and it had a good starting pay with frequent raises available. The job would start in one week. It was a week before my official discharge from the hospital, but I knew if this was God's plan that would not be a problem. I told her I was very interested so she set up an interview for me with the owners. They told me they still had a few other people to interview but would get back to me in two days with their decision.

I never prayed so much in my whole life as I did those next two days. It was exactly what I wanted. It was just what I'd asked the Lord for, but was it what God wanted for me? I was learning what it meant to trust and obey. Marie told me that if I believed this job was what God had for me that I was to thank God for it. I told her I didn't understand how I could thank God for something I didn't have yet. Marie told me that was called "exercising my faith." Faith means you believe you are going to receive what you have prayed for before you actually see it happen.

Two days later the landscaping company called and offered me the job if I still wanted it. I praised the Lord when I heard the news and told them I would indeed take the job. I was convinced that the Lord had heard my prayer, knew the desires of my heart and had honored my faith. Marie, my doctor, and my family were very happy for me. Marie and I knew the job came from God. He was showing me how to walk in faith and to see that He was interested in guiding me in every aspect of my life. Everything was falling into place. I knew God was going to be with me even after I left the hospital. I was not going out into the world alone. My new job would start a week before my discharge and my doctor cleared it with the hospital so I could go to work.

My doctor and my team thought it was best to work from the floor that first week so they could help me through the transition of leaving the hospital and entering the workforce. It would also allow me to attend one more family session with my mother who was the only one left willing to attend. By now she and my family were aware of my sudden trust in God, and my involvement with another church. From the outside it didn't seem to bother them. They were witnessing the change in me and began seeing my life come back together. When I think of all I put them through, I knew they must have been thankful to finally be getting the old Judy back. What they didn't know was that the old Judy had died in the hospital and the Lord was sending a new, though not perfect, Judy out that would be a reflection of His great love.

I still cry every time I think of all the people I said good-bye to those last couple of days before I left the hospital. There were just so many people the Lord used to reach me. What was even harder was saying good-bye to what the hospital had always meant to me. It had played such a large part during one of the most important growth periods in my life. The memories of my stay there will probably not all be written down on paper, but they will forever remain in my heart. All the trials, defeats, triumphs, and victories will always be a part of me. I see now that they were all part of God's plan to bring me home to Him.

I know the only person who can even begin to fathom how I feel about my stay in the hospital is Marie. I believe God provided Marie for a companion for me for that part of my journey toward wholeness. Though I knew that part of my journey was over it was hard to give up all that the hospital, the staff, and Marie meant to me. We talked about that, the separation and anxiety I was feeling, but I knew in my heart it was a step I had to take.

The night before my discharge I lay crying in my bed, pleading with God to make the emptiness and sadness go away. I told Him I knew it would be hard at first but I was willing to say good-bye to the hospital for good. I also knew that in saying good-bye to the hospital, I was also saying good-bye to that sick little girl that had now grown up and was ready to leave the security of the "nest" the hospital had provided for me during that wilderness time of my life. I pleaded with God to not make me give up everything associated with that experience.

"Please God," I cried out, "don't make me give up Marie right now, too."

Living Proof

My family was very apprehensive about having me come home. I couldn't blame them since both times I'd left the hospital before I had ended up right back in. But they were willing to give me the benefit of the doubt that this time would be different. I knew it would be hard to live at home again, especially after having been away for so long. I had to live with their fears about me getting sick again. I tried to reassure them that this time was different. Though they didn't understand why, I knew the Lord had not brought me this far to just drop me off and leave me on my own.

As long as I continued to walk with Him and remembered to surrender everything to Him, I knew this time I was on my way to a lasting victory. I wanted to prove to my family that God was the one who was healing me. Every time I had left the hospital before I had tried to walk it alone, but this time I knew God would be right there with me. I wanted to be living proof that God was the way to live a healthy productive life.

Marie had set up an aftercare plan for me to come back to the hospital once a week to talk with her. I would also be seeing my doctor for outpatient therapy once a week. I decided to have a few more family sessions with my mother after I left to help if any problems arose at home. Everything was in place. I knew it was time for me to move into the next phase of God's plan for my life.

Your Turn

With God in the driver's seat and my heart now His, things began to fall in place. I had joy for the first time in a long time and was motivated to get out of the hospital. Looking for a job, getting ready to say good-bye to my team, giving up my anorexia, and gaining weight were big steps for me, but I attached myself to the Lord and began praying and seeking His best. He was faithful at every turn.

• What are some things that you need to pray to God for in order to take your next step toward wholeness?

Read Matthew 7:9-11:

> *You parents—if your children ask for a loaf of bread, do you give them a stone instead? Or if they ask for a fish, do you give them a snake? Of course not! If you sinful people know how to give good gifts to your children, how much more will your heavenly Father give good gifts to those who ask him.*

Think It Through

Confusion about life's circumstances can be so overwhelming. Being by yourself can cause great fear. This verse compares our earthly father with our heavenly Father. Maybe your earthly father was not very attentive or even around, but your heavenly Father says that He will answer your prayers and give you the best of what you are praying for. I needed to have God's best for me. How about You? Will you trust God in prayer to provide for you as you call on Him today?

Chapter Fifteen: Going Home

On April 24, 1985 I was discharged from the hospital. I drove myself home to spend my first night with my parents. The months of May and June were a time of adjustment as I learned to live as a normal, healthy, functioning member of the family instead of the lonely, depressed, sick girl who used to live there. My mother was especially fearful and seemed to be watching me very closely. My whole family treated me as if I was someone who was very fragile and who could break any moment. They were afraid of sparking my anger which in the past had meant I was getting sick again. I strove to show them it wasn't going to happen this time. I really wanted my life to be a reflection of God's love.

My eating was good at home and I was maintaining my desired weight range but my choices of food began to get repetitious. I had certain "safe foods" that I had grown accustomed to at the hospital. I noticed my mother was worrying about what I ate. I wanted to prove to her that I was indeed getting better so I needed to let go of that behavior.

I did experience a time of emptiness after leaving the hospital, but noticed that it didn't last too long. I faithfully stuck to my outpatient therapy so I was receiving ongoing support from Dr. Fargo, and I talked and visited Marie quite often at the hospital as well. I saw the Lord begin to fill the voids in my life. I loved my job and had an opportunity to share with my friends at work about how the Lord was working in my life. I spent a lot of time with Pastor Brown and his family, receiving counseling and fellowship. I also began to develop an interest in becoming a more active member of the church.

One day the piano player left our church to go to another one, and Pastor Brown asked me if I would consider playing the worship music. I was shocked. I had asked the Lord for an opportunity to use my musical abilities, but so soon? With much fear, I said I would, knowing God knew exactly what I needed to do and when. When I told Marie, she was delighted to see how the Lord was going to use me and offered to help with suggestions for the music.

The time I spent with the Browns was indeed very special to me. For the first time, I was exposed to how a real Christian family applies the statutes of the Lord in their daily walk with Him. Since I didn't have that type of environment at home, it sometimes made living at home difficult. I saw something in that Christian family I had never seen before, and I wanted it in my own family.

I began sharing with my family what I saw and ways I thought would help our family establish a closer walk with Him. This offended my parents and created a lot of friction between us. They had no idea what I was talking about and didn't care to find out. I think they thought that my faith was some kind of phase I was going through to help me overcome my disease. I wanted God to use me to help my family, but I was learning I had to do things His way and in His time and not try to make things happen.

Marie and I would not just talk about how I was doing. She often talked with me about her love of God and her church, and I would talk about mine. We were both amazed at how the Lord had really begun working in many different areas of my life. As Marie talked about the music and all of the activities at her church, I realized that although I had a job and was busy with school, I really had no social life. As I mentioned this to Marie, she shared how important it was to have Christian friends to hang out with.

Friends were one thing I did not have. I did not have any Christian relationships with people my own age. My church was very small in number and everyone was either older or younger than I was. Though the people at my church were very loving and caring, there didn't seem to be much membership growth, especially in my age group. As I began to long for Christian relationships with people my own age, I wondered about the lack of social activities at my church. I discussed my concerns with the Lord and my desire to be where He wanted me to be. I was about to learn that every detail of my life was important to my heavenly Father.

Your Turn

I had not been home to live for any significant amount of time in almost three years. So getting discharged from the hospital, which I had determined was to be my last discharge, was really scary. My family was not quite sure about this God thing that I started to share with them. I knew that I was going home with God for the first time in my life and I also knew God would get me through all of the adjustments. Fear consumed my family and I started to get fearful as well, until I turned to the Lord and remembered He was now driving my life.

• Who is driving your life now? If God is, are you remembering to trust Him with everything in your life? If not, what prevents you from trusting Him now?

___

___

___

Read Psalm 55:22:

> *Give your burdens to the Lord and He will take care of you; He will not permit the godly to slip and fall.*

Think It Through

What an assuring verse about the sustaining power of God in the lives of those who are now walking with Him, instead of against Him! Whatever comes up in your life, you now have a loving Father to go to and tell Him your cares. He says you can give them to Him and He will guide and direct your footsteps. What are the cares that are consuming you today? Won't you take a moment right now and give them to the Lord in prayer?

___

___

___

Chapter Sixteen: Friends at Last

I had a Thursday night off from my classes at the vocational school and decided to go for a drive with my youngest sister. As we were talking, I decided to show her where the school was that I had been attending. However, I made a wrong turn somewhere along the way and suddenly found myself on the wrong road. I was unfamiliar with the area we were in so I decided to find a place to turn around and get back to where I was familiar with the roads. I turned into the parking lot of a little white church to turn around.

All the windows were open and I heard the most beautiful singing coming out of that little church. As I sat there listening, I decided I wanted to get closer so I pulled the car up as close as I could and then got out of the car. My sister looked at me like I was out of my mind and wanted to know what I was doing.

I said, "I have got to get out. I have got to hear more of this wonderful singing."

I had never heard anything like it before. It had a contemporary beat and I could hear tambourines coming out of that tiny little country church. I looked at the plaque next to the front door that gave the name of the church. It gave the times of the services. I wrote everything down, hopped back in my car and headed for home. I couldn't wait to call Marie and tell her about this amazing little church I had stumbled across.

Marie had been encouraging me to look for a church that had more to offer someone my age. Her only guidelines were that I find one that preaches and teaches the Bible. She knew I needed to develop Christian friendships. As soon as I got home I called Marie and asked her if she knew anything about this church that I found. When I told her the name of it, she was quiet for a moment.

“That’s my church,” she said quietly.

“You have got to be kidding me,” I laughed, “You mean to tell me that out of all the churches in the area that I could have stumbled upon, I end up at your church?”

I suddenly remembered there was something about patient /nurse relationships that didn’t allow her to invite me to attend her church.

“Does that mean I can’t go to that church?” I asked.

“No, you found it yourself. God led you there. It is like a miracle!” she said excitedly.

I started to attend there on Thursday night and Sunday morning. I figured I could still attend Pastor Brown’s church on Sunday afternoon. The first time I ever walked into this new church was on a Thursday night. I was greeted by a very tall man. He had to be over six foot tall. He welcomed me and introduced himself as Steve Roberts. Little did I know that I would date and eventually become life partners with him.

Marie told me about the singles’ group and I found out Steve was in the group as well. Steve introduced me to a bunch of people and I started going to the singles’ group on a regular basis.

In the months of July and August, the Browns went away to various Christian camps to teach. They knew there was a lot of tension at my home as my life became more and more centered around my relationship with the Lord. As much as I wanted to be a witness to my family, when the Browns asked me if I would be interested in house-sitting while they were away at camp, I accepted. I was a little apprehensive at the thought of being by myself for two months, but I really believed the Lord wanted me to have this time just with Him.

I was concerned that not having others around to prove anything to might cause me to start digressing into my old habits, but I realized it was time to advance to the next level of faith. I needed time to learn I could totally lean on the Lord for my strength and win this battle against my control issues and this disease.

I was beginning to feel right at home at this new church. The worship was uplifting as young and old openly praised the Lord. I felt close to the Lord as I joined in with their worship. The pastor preached the Word of God with great power and truth. The people were wonderful and I saw all my new friends from the singles' group there, too. I knew I wanted to be a part of that body of believers; I just didn't know how to tell the Browns.

How to Win

The time alone house-sitting for the Browns proved to be a wonderful time of discovery for me. I really enjoyed getting into music and even started writing my own songs—something I had never done before. I started painting again and found a great inner peace and joy as I watched what I was able to express through my drawings. The Browns had hoped I would use the time alone to draw closer to the Lord, and I did through my music and my paintings.

They left me a book about loneliness. It really spoke to my heart about where I was in the world. I was lonely because my family and I didn't share the same interest and love for the Lord and because I had no Christian friends. I was still seeing my doctor and Marie on a regular basis and spoke with each of them about the loneliness I was experiencing. I spent a lot of time reading my Bible and talking with the Lord. I took my loneliness issues to Him, knowing He would know exactly what I needed.

A week before the Browns were scheduled to return, I found I had a lot of things to talk with God about. Before they had left for camp, the Browns had invited me to live with them on a permanent basis and asked me to pray about it while they were gone. I had always wanted to be a part of a real Christian family that could guide me in the ways of the Lord, something my own family could not do. When they returned I talked with Pastor Brown and his wife about my desire to live with them but also my conflicting feelings about where I wanted to go to church. I felt it might be a problem if I lived living there and went to a different fellowship so I had decided it would be better for me to go back home.

Pastor Brown patiently listened as I shared my heart with him and then told me it wasn't because I attended the same church as they did that they had invited me to live with them. He said they loved me, not because of where I worshipped but because of who I was. They loved me as a fellow Christian and encouraged me to stay even if I decided to attend the new church. I was truly amazed that these people loved me with no strings attached. They offered to help me consider the situation based purely on what God wanted me to do. Then we talked about the pros and cons of living with them versus living at home. They encouraged me to pray about it before I made a final decision.

I asked the Lord to show me where He wanted me to live and after much prayer, He began speaking to my heart that I needed to return home. I felt He was assuring me that the Christian family I so longed for I would get, but it wouldn't be with the Browns. Of course I questioned this and didn't understand what Christian family He was referring to. However, I obeyed the Lord and told the Browns what I felt the Lord was telling me to do.

Your Turn

Being home for the first time in a long time, I had lost touch with so many of my old friends. I was lonely and in need of some new friends that shared my love of the Lord. I wanted my family to embrace my new love of God, but they did not. The Brown family became my instant Christian family and I thought moving in with them was an answer to prayer. However, I lacked peace with that decision and something was pulling me back home to my family. With a lot of prayer and counsel, I knew what I had to do.

• Has your destructive behavior from the past cost you relationships? If so, what are you doing to make new ones?

___

___

___

Read Matthew 5:14, 16:

> *You are the light of the world—like a city on a mountain, glowing in the night for all to see.....In the same way, let your good deeds shine out for all to see, so that everyone will praise your heavenly Father."*

Think it Through

When you allow Jesus to take the steering wheel of your life, you enter into a transforming relationship with Him. This verse compares your life to that of a light. We are instructed to let it shine and not hide it. You can now be an influence in the lives of those around you that may be in a place of despair as you have been. Who do you know who could benefit from a loving relationship with God? Will you share your God story with them this week?

___

___

___

Chapter Seventeen: Yes, to His Plan!

Now I knew where the Lord wanted me to live, but I was even more convinced He also wanted me to attend this new church. He had opened the door for a reason so I walked through it. What I saw on the one side was a bigger vision of what the Lord could do as the Brown's church continued to grow and mature. At the same time I realized why He had moved me into a mature body of believers where I could witness the Lord's work as well as receive instruction for the work I was faced with at home. The Lord once again proved He saw my needs before I was even aware of them, and assured me that as I kept doing what He was telling me to do, He would provide exactly what I needed.

As I started to attend Marie's church, I saw our patient-nurse relationship slowly fade away and a new one begin to unfold. Although my aftercare with her at the hospital was over, that was not to be the end of our relationship. I saw her in church and we talked quite frequently on the phone. She introduced me to my new church family as well as to my new pastor. She helped me get involved in this new church by literally dragging me to every function. Her efforts and support made it easier to get to know my new church family and to find what God had in mind, for not only my instruction but my service to Him.

I had been seeing Dr. Fargo once a week, but as I grew in faith and confidence in the Lord, I decided to begin seeing him every other week. As I drew closer to the Lord and the people at the church, I began drifting away from my doctor. I would always be grateful for this man who had seen me through the worst times in my life and had always been there when I needed him. I realized he was now becoming less and less of an influence in my life as God was becoming more and more.

My new pastor was preaching about the conflict ungodly counsel from non-believers would cause in our lives. When the pastor focused in on psychiatry, I was offended. I had received so much from Dr. Fargo and the staff at the hospital, but I saw the Lord was using the pastor to speak to me about my dependency on those who did not have the same belief system I did. I had never even thought about giving up Dr. Fargo, but I knew if I was to follow in the ways of the Lord that I would soon have to let him go. I couldn't see how I could do this; I had developed such a love for him. Marie said to give it over to the Lord and ask Him to prepare my heart for the time I knew would soon be coming. During the following month, He did just that.

In October of 1985, I went to Dr. Fargo to tell him I wanted to stop therapy. I told him that I felt I didn't need treatment with him any longer. I know that he knew as well as I did that it wasn't my two sessions a month with him that was helping me get better. But it was as hard for him to let go of me as it was for me to let go of him. We couldn't deny the remarkable progress I had made since I had been discharged from the hospital. I don't think he was totally convinced that the credit belonged to the Lord, but I knew only God could have done such a complete makeover.

I told him the time had come for me to totally trust the Lord as my physician. He looked doubtful but supported me as long as this was my own decision. He was honest about his concerns and reminded me that most patients with eating disorders remained in therapy for years, and that only five percent actually had a complete recovery and lived normal lives. An alarming 75% remained in and out of therapy and hospitals pretty much all their lives. I knew what he said was true, but I also knew something he did not. He was referring to those who were healed by the worldly process of doctors and hospitals. What I had was the divine and perfect physician, Jesus. He had a perfect success rate!

I was very sad leaving his office that day and felt as though I were experiencing a death that needed to be mourned. It was a death to the past and all my old worldly support systems, but I knew they had been replaced with a new living relationship with the Lord. I was learning to lean on the Lord for all of my needs, each and every day.

Learning to Lean on Him

I never thought I could give up Dr. Fargo and live to tell the story, but the Lord is faithful. He prepared my heart for that day so I would be ready when He said I was ready, not when I thought I was ready. The Lord never leaves anyone empty. When He removes one thing from our lives, He replaces it with something more wonderful. I saw Him begin to fill that emptiness I had lived with for so much of my life with more of Him through Marie and my relationships with the people at my new church. Marie was no longer just my nurse; now she was also my sister in the Lord.

I saw a lot of growth begin to take place in my life during this time. I was really learning to totally lean on the Lord for solutions to all my problems and find help in dealing with all of my fears. I still had eating problems, but I trusted God and saw my eating habits become less ritualized. I found I could eat things I used to avoid. I also began developing closer relationships with some of the singles at my new church and started to have a very busy social life.

Things started to go so well I was shocked when one day I got on the scale and discovered my weight had gone beyond the weight range I had so faithfully kept to since I had left the hospital. It was not a lot of weight gain, but it was enough to make me panic. In the past I would have tried to take control of the situation myself and just stop eating to lose the weight, but this time I knew the Lord was in control of every area of my life—including what the scale was telling me. With counseling from Marie I began to realize God's plan was not to make me fat, but that He could be testing my faith.

Every trial we encounter in life is to increase our faith in Him. It was time for me to see if I had truly given control of my life to Him. This was an area I had always wanted to control in the past and had found difficult to submit to God. I prayed once again and gave complete control of the situation to the Lord. Instead of going without food, I made a conscious effort to try foods I had never allowed myself to eat before. It was one thing to say I believed and trusted in God but it was quite another to put actions to those words. I had recently learned that "faith without works is dead" (see James 2:26), and I was determined to act on that faith. As I gave this situation to the Lord, it freed my mind to focus on important things such as my job situation.

I was still working as an interior landscaper which involved working with one other person to maintain an established route of accounts after an initial installation had been completed. We were on our own during the day and would have to keep a log of our time spent at each account, then hand it in to our supervisor once a week for billing purposes. This placed a lot of responsibility on each of us to record our time honestly. We had gotten our routes down to such a pattern that the time spent at each account became shorter which left us with extra time. We started taking one and two hour lunch breaks. We were only scheduled for a half an hour, but figured if our work was done we were entitled to a longer lunch.

Well, I knew you could compromise rules in the world and get away with it, but I was soon to realize the Lord wouldn't stand for compromise with His laws. It wasn't long before the Spirit of the Lord began to convict my heart. Here I was sharing my newfound faith in Lord and how He was changing me with the other girls at work, yet I was doing the same dishonest things they were. As I grew in the knowledge of the things of God, I realized the company itself was doing some things that compromised the laws of the Lord. God was opening my eyes to see things from His point of view, and I found that everywhere I turned I was doing things I knew would not please Him in order to keep my job. I told myself I needed this job, but the lack of peace in my heart told me I needed to leave.

Our pastor had recently taught about integrity in our Christian walk with the Lord. I knew that I needed to leave my job because there were areas within the company where they were asking me not to be honest. I really liked it there so I prayed about it. I talked to Marie about what was going on and how I felt the Lord wanted me to quit, but I didn't know where I was supposed to find work if I did.

Marie felt that maybe it was the Lord leading me away from there to pursue a career as a dental assistant. She knew it would be hard for me to leave the security of that job, but reminded me it was God who gave me that job in the first place. He could certainly take it away and move me into another. Marie assured me that the Lord knew the situation and would be faithful to supply me with an open door somewhere else. It was my responsibility to trust and obey.

I stepped out in faith and quit that job. I told my parents I felt the Lord was calling me in a different direction, but they didn't understand. To tell you the truth, I really couldn't blame them. Here I was with school loans and car insurance to pay not to mention my need for good health insurance, and I was quitting a job without another one to go to. However, I knew that the peace I felt after quitting was a sign I was doing the right thing. I found a Scripture that helped me stay true to what I believed God was telling me to do (Proverbs 3:5-6).

> *Trust in the Lord with all of your heart, and lean not on your own understanding; in all your ways acknowledge Him, and He shall direct your paths. (NKJV)*

Your Turn

Living home now, I really drew closer to the Lord. Decisions to leave therapy with my doctor, attending a new church, and job issues, were enough to keep me tied to God. I prayed about everything. I was learning to trust and obey Him. I began to flourish.

• In what areas of your life do you need to trust and lean on God more?

____

____

____

____

____

____

Read Proverbs 3:5-6:

> *Trust in the Lord with all of your heart, and lean not on your own understanding; in all your ways acknowledge Him, and He shall direct your paths. (NKJV)*

Think It Through

Getting lost is a terrible feeling. It is great that we have devices like the GPS to help us when we need guidance on how to get where we need to go. This verse, simply put, tells us to trust in the Lord. Lean on Him in every area of your life and trust that He will guide you to where He wants you to be. In what area of your life do you feel lost and alone and confused? Try bringing it to the Lord and listen for His guidance as you read His Word and pray.

____

____

____

Chapter Eighteen: Staying the Course

I quit my job at the landscaping company at the end of September knowing it would be next to impossible to look for another job while I was still working there. My parents didn't approve, but I was totally giving this situation to the Lord. I can't tell you how scared I was during this time of unemployment. Even though I felt a peace about the situation, people around me told me I had made too hasty a decision. I really had to fight the doubt that tried to cause confusion in my mind.

The first week of unemployment proved to be a time of diligently searching through the want ads and setting up job interviews with various dental offices in the area. I would go to the interviews with great faith and believe the Lord would open the door for me. But after each interview, I would pray and ask the Lord to close that door. Now that might sound a bit contradictory. I believed I was supposed to be looking for a job in the dental health field, but after visiting so many dental offices, the hope and enthusiasm I had felt while I was taking the course wasn't there anymore. I couldn't understand why so I prayed even more.

"Okay, God, I know I took that course for a reason and borrowed five hundred dollars from my parents to do it (which I still owe them by the way), but I don't have a desire to follow through with this as a career," I told God, "So what is going on? Is it me and my fear or is it You telling me not to pursue this direction?"

Then I asked the Lord, "If it is me, then please give me back the desire to follow Your plan, but if it is You directing me away from this field, then lead me to where it is You would have me to be."

By the end of the first week I had become very discouraged and began to question the Lord. "Why did You allow me to take that course if You didn't want me to use it? Why was the money that wasn't there suddenly provided so I could take the course? Why did I have to leave my other job only to be left without a job now?"

I had more questions than answers, but I continued to pray and do all that I knew to do. As I faithfully did my part, I soon learned the path the Lord was preparing me to follow.

My older sister was working for the school district as a teaching assistant and just loved her job. She had been working with young children but had recently switched to a position in the junior high school. I called her at the beginning of my second week of unemployment and told her of my job search. I told her I was getting discouraged and she suggested I try applying at the school district as a teaching assistant. I asked her what the requirements were and she said all I needed were six college credits. I had fifteen credits and as she described the job to me, it reawakened in me the desire to help others though I had never considered working with children.

Why not, I thought to myself, *I'm still just a kid myself, but I have learned a lot from what I have been through. Maybe what I have learned along the way could help other kids going through similar situations.*

The more we talked, the more I liked the idea. She encouraged me to talk with our neighbor who was in charge of the special education department for the school district. He would know if there were any job openings. It seemed like a long shot and like there were a lot of things against me—like my age, lack of experience with children, and the fact that the school year was already in session. Still I couldn't eliminate the possibility until I had at least tried. Every time I tried to talk myself out of calling our neighbor, I lost my peace. I finally called, feeling the Lord had pointed me in this direction.

As I explained my situation, my neighbor asked me to come in and fill out an application. He told me he knew of two recent job openings in the district and said he could probably send me out on the interviews as soon as he had my paperwork. I hung up and cried in amazement at how faithful the Lord was. He had shown me again how He was fully aware of my situation and already had the solution in place. I just needed to lift my needs up to Him and be open to His plan, whether it matched up with mine or not.

I praised the Lord and thanked Him for His love and faithfulness. I somehow knew the job was mine though I had no idea what school I would be working in or what age group He would have me work with. I was interviewed by two schools—one was a junior high and the other was an early childhood program working with developmentally delayed children ages two to four. I wanted to work with the older children because I felt I had more to offer them, but I waited to hear from either school to see where the Lord was going to send me. Within a day of the interviews I was called by the early childhood program and offered the job which I immediately accepted.

Blessings from the Lord

I was so excited. I was to start the first week of October but in the meantime there were forms to fill out as well as a meeting to attend that would explain my salary and benefits. In all the excitement of making the calls and going to the interviews as the Lord had so obviously directed, I had never asked about the pay or the benefits. When I went to fill out the forms, the lady explained the pay and how the benefits package worked. I was totally shocked! The job I had accepted had many blessing from the Lord all wrapped up in one package.

The salary was more than I had ever made before with yearly raises, plus I belonged to a union which entitled me to discounts at various stores in the area. I had medical and dental insurance, paid sick days, and the same vacation days as the children. I also had the summer off if I wanted it. But what really got me were the hours. I would work from eight in the morning until three in the afternoon, but the children would only be there from nine until two. I realized the Lord knew I could really only tolerate a short workday at this point in my recovery.

So in less than three weeks after quitting my landscaping job, I began working as a teaching assistant with developmentally delayed children. I worked with another assistant and a fantastic teacher. There were ten children in my class, each with a different need. They were not all physically disabled, but most had speech or behavioral problems. Many of them came from very dysfunctional family environments and this school was a haven of security, growth and enjoyment for them, providing what they were not getting at home.

It was certainly not a regular nine to five job. It was actually a lot of fun working with the kids. I was able to use my art and creative abilities as well as play the piano during music time. Don't get me wrong; it was not all fun and games. The children were often very demanding and required a lot of special attention. Some days they would drive me up a wall, but all I had to do was remind myself all these children really needed was to be loved. I could give them the love that was lacking in their lives.

I found it was truly an opportunity to see the Lord working through me. He was developing patience in me as well as a love for those less fortunate than myself. Sometimes I would get frustrated when I looked at some of these kids and realized how much they needed to know God. I just wanted to take them aside and tell each one of them about a God that loved them more than anyone they had ever known. Working in the city school district didn't allow for any talk about the Lord, but I knew He would use me to make a difference in their young lives.

Although I couldn't speak directly about God, the Lord gave me an opportunity to demonstrate His great love to these children through my daily interaction with them. I went to work every day determined to really shine forth His love through me. I made mistakes along the way, but the Lord used it all to continue to develop godly character in me.

Sometimes I think about all the Lord has brought me through and I wonder if He ever looked at me as being developmentally delayed. I do know though that He placed me there to teach me more about His great love as I worked to help those children. I also know my schooling will never end. I'm in His school for life.

Your Turn

In a marathon, it is crucial to train your body and your mind for the race ahead. Pacing and having a great trainer by your side are everything. I was running in the marathon of my recovery toward wholeness and the people God had put in place to train me were everywhere. I had Marie, my doctor, Pastor Brown and his family, as well as my pastor from my church. Even with all that, my main coach was the Lord Himself. Notice how many times I went to the Lord with the issues that came my way, and each time His guidance showed me the way to success.

•Who is walking with you through your road to wholeness?

____

____

____

• Are you making God the lead coach in your life?

____

____

____

Read Matthew 19:26:

> *Humanly speaking it is impossible. But with God everything is possible.*

Think it Through

The major lead in my life was being given to the Lord. This Scripture says that man cannot be our all in all, but that with God *all things* are possible. I made it up and out of the place I was in, and you can, too.

Begin your journey today and make Him your all in all. Turn the steering wheel of your life over to Him as I did and He will be faithful. What do you have to lose?

____

____

____

Your Story

Today's Date: ____________________

These are the things I need to pray about in order to take my next step toward wholeness:

These are the cares that are still causing me confusion and fear:

These things are keeping me from trusting God and turning the steering wheel of my life over to Him:

These are the people that could benefit from hearing about my God story:

Conclusion: All is Forgiven

Today I feel the Lord wants me to be unique in His ways,
not mine, and certainly not the world's.
Help me, Lord, to honor this. I love you!
~ *Judy*

It's now March of 1986 and as I sit here rereading this testimony, I realize how inadequately I have described all that the Lord has brought me through. I am one month away from my one year anniversary of being out of the hospital. This is the longest time I've ever been out. This past year has been one of almost complete recovery from the eating and behavior problems I have dealt with nearly all my life. I say almost because I know the Lord allows certain remnants to remain to be used to continually draw me closer to Him and to remind me to always look up.

Along with all my physical victories, the Lord has blessed me with a wonderful church family and pastor to help guide me in my Christian journey. He has opened doors for me to be a light for Him at work, and although my family still does not know the Lord as I do, I feel He is using me to shine His light to them. I believe with my whole heart that He will draw each and every one of my family members to Him and that God has placed me there for His purposes.

The Lord has provided for my every need since I've accepted His control for my life. He has opened doors I never knew existed. He has allowed me to draw close to people of all ages at my new church and has put me among fellow believers who can counsel me. I know in my heart that the Lord will enable me to give more of myself back to my new church as they have done so much for me.

I praise the Lord every day that when I called out to Him to allow me to keep my relationship with Marie, He heard. The work He has done through her to guide me and to be there for me is something I'll never understand. I love the Lord for giving me Marie! I pray that someday I can give back to her all the love and support she has given me. The Lord has used her in a powerful way to touch and share my journey as I came out of the depths and moved toward wholeness. Words will never give justice to how truly thankful I am to my Lord for Marie.

The words recording my journey this far are all down on paper and my heart rejoices at the realization of how far I have come. However, I also know this is an unfinished story. I say unfinished because I know the Lord will never be finished with me. I am confident that there will be many more God stories to write in the future about trials, failures, and victories which lie ahead as I journey toward wholeness in Him. I no longer face the future with fear. Any time fear tries to push back into my life, I just look back and see how far He has brought me. As I look at my life today, I can't help but look up and know in my heart that "all is forgiven." No matter where I go from here I can believe His promise of His presence with me:

> *And be sure of this: I am with you always, even to the end of the age (Matthew 28:20).*

Epilogue: My Daddy's Heart

I see myself more and more like my father every day.
He's the person I admire most in the world right now
and he's the one that is the hardest
for me to help to understand.
~ Judy

After the first week back from Pastor Brown's house things began to make sense. I saw what the Lord had in mind. He wanted to use me as a light in my own home with my own family. I was to be a witness and living proof of His love. He was also teaching me to trust Him; and He would change my family into the family He desired for me.

I knew it would take some time and a total commitment on my part to develop that light within me that would eventually attract my family to my Lord and Savior. Talk about being faced with a challenge! I truly saw the Lord working in my family as He worked in me, molding me into a light worth shining, especially with my dad.

On April 25, 1986, my one year anniversary of being out of the hospital, I took the day off from school to celebrate. I was home alone playing the piano when my father came in. He was a salesman and he had come home for some lunch.

He heard the piano and asked me, "What are you doing home?"

"Dad, it's my one year anniversary. I've been out of the hospital for one whole year. I decided to take the day off from school to celebrate. Mom gave me a card with your name on it, didn't you know?" I said, laughing.

"Oh, yes, of course I knew. I will be back in a little while," he said as he headed for the door.

About an hour later, I figured he must be home because I heard him back in the kitchen. I didn't think anything of it until he came looking for me. He handed me a card and a box wrapped in aluminum foil. I opened up the card first. It was a beautiful card that gave glory to the Lord. He wrote that he and my Mom just wanted me to know they knew God was doing something amazing in my life. I still have the card. Teary eyed, I opened up the box and inside was a very thin, petite, gold cross with a diamond chip in the middle. I wore that cross every single day. What a special gift he gave me that day along with the hope that his heart was softening towards the things of God.

Heart Surgery

When my father went in for his checkup a few weeks later, they discovered he needed surgery for his heart. He'd had other surgeries before but one day after we found out about this one, he came home after work early. I was back from work and saw him when he walked in. He looked kind of funny so I asked him if something was the matter. This was in June of 1986.

He just looked at me and said, "I'm scared."

I asked him, "What are you afraid of? Are you afraid of dying?"

He shook his head and said, "Yes."

I had been asking the Lord to give me an opportunity to talk with my dad before he went in for this surgery.

"Like I told you before," I said, "you don't need to be afraid to die if you know where you are going to go. Do you know where you are going to go?"

He said, "Well, I hope I go to heaven."

I knew that was my opening. I took the opportunity to share the good news of Jesus making a way for us to heaven with Him again. It was just him and me, sitting in the kitchen talking about the Lord. I know that the

Lord had been working on him and I'll never forget how the Lord gave me that wonderful time with my dad. Did I ever hear my father say he was turning the steering wheel of his life over to God? No, but I did see my father do and say things that were out of his character, and I knew it was God showing me that He was doing something in my father's life.

On Father's Day, I gave him a poem I had written and then I asked him if he would take a walk with me up to the reservoir. He surprised me by saying he wanted to do just that. We took it easy as we walked the mile and half around the reservoir together. It gave me a chance to talk to him about the things God was doing in my life. It was amazing! It was like being at the Mount of Transfiguration (see Matthew 17:2). I didn't want to come down. I finally had my dad all to myself after so many years. I had his undivided attention, something I had been craving for so long. God used that month of June to really convince me that I was where He wanted me to be—home, and that He was at work in my father's heart.

I was working as a teaching assistant and school was almost over, but the Lord told me to take my week's vacation early. He wanted me to spend that time with my dad as he was recovering from his surgery and still in the hospital, so I obeyed. Steve and I were dating at the time, but he was gone that week so I spent a lot of time with my dad. I would go to see him every day and spend most of the day with him. We talked about the Lord and talked about my relationship with Steve. I told my dad I knew I was going to marry Steve. My father smiled at me and said he knew it too.

I discovered that when my dad packed his things to bring to the hospital, he packed the Bible I had given him at Christmas time, an Easter card I had given him that had the whole plan of salvation written out on it, and the poem I had written for him on Father's Day.

One day when I came to visit him, my dad told me some pastor had come up to talk to him. When I asked him if it was a priest, he said no, the man was a pastor but he didn't get the man's name. Dad said they talked about a lot of things that day. I still don't know who that pastor was, but I thank the Lord for him because I could plainly see something had happened that day in my dad's heart.

My dad was still in the hospital for my birthday so Steve took me for a quick celebration and gave me a beautiful necklace. I took off the necklace my dad had given me and wore the new necklace when I went to see my dad later that day.

When I showed my dad what Steve had given me for my birthday, his response was, "Oh, look how easily I was replaced."

I went home and immediately put the cross my dad had given me back on. Three days later my dad died of pneumonia. I think I have only worn that cross maybe five more times since that day because I don't want to lose it. It is such a wonderful reminder of my daddy's heart.

Miracles

Out of all my siblings, I was sitting at the foot of his bed reading to him out of the Bible the night my father went into cardiac arrest. My mother was there, too, sitting next to him. They put him on life support around eight that night and at four the next morning, he passed away. We all had time to go in and talk to him. All of his brothers and sisters came and everybody was encouraging him to fight to live. When I went in for what turned out to be the last time, I told him Jesus was with him and if he was ready to go, to just take the Lord's hand and go.

For me to have been able to say that to my dad was a miracle in itself. I had always said to my doctor that if my father ever died, I didn't know if I would make it. I just never thought I could get through anything like that and being such a young Christian at the time too. It would have been so easy to blame God for it and walk away from the Lord, but God had so prepared my heart that it actually drew me closer to Him.

That all happened just a little over one year after I was discharged from the hospital. I had wanted to be in a Christian home, part of a Christian family, and be accepted as a Christian so much that I almost accepted the Browns' offer to live with them. I am so thankful I had learned early to listen to and trust the Lord when He told me not to live with the Browns but to go back home. I would have missed those nine months with my dad.

Within ten hours of my father's death, I was told by several of my family members that I was the one who killed him. They said I had scared him to death by talking so much about God and dying. In their grief, my mother and my older sister blamed me. However, God had placed me in a really good support system. With my pastor and my new church family, Steve, and Pastor Brown, I was able to ride out the wave of grief and pain caused by not only my father's death, but my family's placement of blame on me.

This is the poem I gave my dad for Father's Day. We had it read at his funeral and the funeral parlor wanted a copy of it which they put it in their foyer.

Come and Play, Daddy

Oh, those days of my childhood
seem to pass quickly in the night,
but the ever vivid memories have
never vanished from my sight.

Though I fondly think
of things we used to do
I know those days are gone,
but we still have me and you.

I know you've watched me grow
and change from day to day,
but I have a secret part of me
that has never gone away.

For there is a little girl, Daddy,
still inside, and she's free

Out of the Depths

and I hear her calling daily.
"Daddy, come play with me."
Let's run again, let's laugh again,
let's play hide and seek.
Will you take me for a ride?
Will you sing me to sleep?

Oh, how she calls you and how
often you don't hear,
that the little girl that calls you
is so very, very near.

Oh, Dad I've watched you grow
and change from day to day,
But did you keep a secret part of you
or did you let it slip away?

Oh, I know there is a secret man
that you keep locked deep inside,
though from others you conceal him.
Well, from me you can not hide.

For like me, you've kept a secret part
of yourself tucked so far away.
The only difference between us
is I'm letting mine come out to play.

For there is a little girl, Daddy,
still inside and she's free,
and I hear her calling daily
"Daddy, come play with me."

All my love, and God's blessing,
Judy
(Written June 15,1986 for Father's Day. Dad died June 30,1986.)

Parents are the pride of their children (Proverbs 17:6b).

Side Note:

My dad's cardiologist was horrified that he had died unexpectedly and wanted to do an autopsy to find out why, but my family would not allow it. I had a dream about Dad's cardiologist about three years later. In the dream I was in his office telling him that God had forgiven him, and that nobody blamed him for my father's death. I told Steve about my dream. He suggested I call my mother and get his name. My aunt had told me that the cardiologist had never done the surgery again after my father died. I made an appointment and Steve and I went to see him. I am sure he was wondering what I could possibly want three years after my father's death.

I sat across from him at his desk and told him God had given me a dream and I shared it with him. Then I told him that I just wanted him to know that I knew my father's death was not his fault. I explained that I had learned that God has our days numbered, and He knows everything about when we are to be born and when we are to die. He looked at me with tears in his eyes and told me he had stopped doing the surgery after my father died. Then he shared that out of all the surgeries he had done and of all the people he had lost, that my dad's death was the one that baffled and hurt him the most. It was shortly after that he started doing his surgeries again. I believe God touched his life that day and I am so glad God sent me to talk with the doctor.

Your Father knows exactly what you need even before you ask him (Matthew 6:8b).

Your Turn

God knew I needed to be home. He gave me precious time with my earthly father that I had never had before. I was able to share with him before he died how by giving God the steering wheel of my life, I was now able to keep my anorexia in check, and how God was piecing my life together. I would have never thought my father would die so suddenly, but God knew and took care of every detail. I loved my father and I know where he is and I will someday be reunited with him. Without God, I am confident that I would have fallen back into the pit of despair that He had pulled me from. My decision in February to give my life to God was a turning point in my life.

Read Matthew 5:4:

God blesses those who mourn, for they will be comforted.

Think it Through

Life is full of unknowns; yet when you walk with God, He is able to walk with you through everything and meet you where you are. Terrible things can happen like accidents, death, and disease, but we have a God who knows our pain. In this verse He promises to bring comfort to those who are in a place of deep sadness or depression and hurt. He brought His comfort to me with the passing of my father and He is there for you.

Can you reach up to your heavenly Father and receive His comfort in those areas of your life where you need it most?

If you have not already done so, why not make sure you know where you are going should you die today. Pray this prayer and turn your life over once and for all to your loving Heavenly Father:

Lord, I admit that I am sinner and that I have done things that are displeasing to You. I ask for forgiveness and for You to come into my heart, take the steering wheel of my life, and bring Your Holy Spirit to guide and direct me. I thank You for sending Your Son, Jesus, who was willing to die on the cross for me and take my punishment upon Himself. I gratefully look forward to the days ahead of getting to know You more personally. Amen

Your Story

Today is the day I asked God to forgive me and take control of my life:

Today I begin writing my new story:

Father in Heaven

Father in heaven
See your daughter's heart below
And know that in your arms
Is the place I long to go

As a silver haired father
Once held his daughter in his arms
I know that place with You
Is sheltered from all harm

And as a silver haired father
Once spoke softly to her ear
Your voice with likewise calmness
Assures me not to fear

This is a place of quiet peacefulness
Where I am near and in your grace
And restfulness engulfs me
As I lay in Your embrace

An unlike my silver haired father
Who now with You, once held me near
I know Your arms eternal
Will never disappear

~ Judy Roberts, 1986

A Note from the Author

This book has taken you through my initial battle with anorexia and how the Lord showed Himself faithful as I began my journey toward wholeness. But this book records only the beginning of a life filled with God stories. There is so much more I could share about how He faithfully guided me through marriage, infertility, and adoption. He has been my source of strength when my husband and I experienced great financial success, and then devastating disaster as our world was seemingly torn apart by a nearly fatal accident that almost took my husband's life.

If you would like to contact me for more information, please visit my website: www.gracetomove.com.

More Titles by 5 Fold Media

Why Me, O Lord
by Melissa Calegan
$15.00
ISBN: 978-1-936578-01-6

"That young, desperate, lost, lonely girl was really me. I almost ended my life before it really even began. Yes, I was a different person. I had not yet met the man that would save my life, my Savior, Jesus. Question after question, issue after issue, time after time, I asked, 'Why me, O Lord?' "

Why Me, O Lord by Melissa Calegan is a journey to the deepest pits of anger, abandonment, resentment, depression and suicide, then finally to freedom and joy. The author walks the reader through her testimony where she discovers that answers can be found.

The Psalms, Poetry on Fire
The Passion Translation
by Dr. Brian Simmons
$19.00
ISBN: 978-1-936578-28-3

The Psalms, Poetry on Fire translated by Dr. Brian Simmons find the words that express our deepest and strongest emotions. The Psalms will turn your sighing into singing and your trouble into triumph. No matter what you may be going through in your life, the Psalms have a message for you! As you read these 150 poetic masterpieces, your heart will be stirred to worship God in greater ways.

Author Brian Simmons shares, "The Psalms are meant to do to you what they did to David; they will bring you from your cave of despair into the glad presence of the King who likes you just the way you are." It truly is Poetry on Fire!

Like 5 Fold Media on Facebook, follow us on Twitter!

CPSIA information can be obtained at www.ICGtesting.com
Printed in the USA
BVOW012257070513

320147BV00004B/7/P